"The key word in this title is *community*—we need towns and cities efficient enough to slow down global warming and durable enough to ride out what we can't prevent. What a handy guide for getting started!"

—Bill McKibben, author, *The Bill McKibben Reader*

"If you have been looking for a way to do your part to create a sustainable future, look no further. This book is as good as it gets—a concise guide to personal actions that can make a huge difference when combined with the actions of others. Read it and put its suggestions into effect."

—Dan Chiras is a green building consultant, public speaker, teacher, and author of numerous books on green building and residential renewable energy, including *The Homeowner's Guide to Renewable Energy*, *The New Ecological Home*, and *The Solar House*.

"Global warming is the most urgent challenge facing the inhabitants of Earth today. The solutions are greater energy efficiencies and utilization of clean, renewable energy sources. In *Go Green*, Nancy Taylor has provided a tremendous public service in offering a highly useful easy-to-understand menu of choices we can all implement as we take major steps toward combating global warming and leading the way toward a healthy, safe, sustainable future."

—Rocky Anderson, former mayor of Salt Lake City

"If you've seen the movie, heard the lecture, and read all the reasons why you should be scared witless about global warming, here's what you can actually do about it—read Nancy Taylor's book. It's short, succinct, well-organized, practical, and upbeat."

—Robert Collier, visiting scholar, Center for Environmental Public Policy, University of California at Berkeley

"The world is a better place because Nancy Taylor is in it. In this much-needed and most welcome book, Taylor provides simple, clear stories about powerful ways we can change our daily lives to leave the world of the future better than that of the past."

—Devra Davis, PhD, MPH, Director of the Center for Environmental Oncology, University of Pittsburgh Cancer Institute, Professor, Department of Epidemiology, Graduate School of Public Health

"This is an empowering book that can make a real difference to your life and your planet. It offers a practical and visionary, effective, detailed and compassionate way to live green."

—Jack Kornfield, founder of Spirit Rock Meditation Center, author of *A Path with Heart*

GO

Green

How to Build an
Earth-Friendly Community

NANCY H. TAYLOR

Gibbs Smith, Publisher
TO ENRICH AND INSPIRE HUMANKIND
Salt Lake City | Charleston | Santa Fe | Santa Barbara

To my beautiful daughters,
Margaret Ann Davis
and Andrea Taylor Davis,
and to all the children of the earth.

• • • • •

First Edition
12 11 10 09 08   5 4 3 2

Published by
Gibbs Smith, Publisher
P.O. Box 667
Layton, Utah 84041

Orders: 1.800.835.4993
www.gibbs-smith.com

Designed by Glyph Publishing Arts
Printed and bound in Canada

Library of Congress Cataloging-in-Publication Data

Taylor, Nancy H.
  Go green : how to build an earth-friendly community / Nancy H. Taylor. — 1st
ed.
     p. cm.
  Includes bibliographical references and index.
  ISBN-13: 978-1-4236-0387-0
  ISBN-10: 1-4236-0387-7
  1. Green movement. 2. Political ecology. 3. Environmental policy.
4. Nature—Effect of human beings on. I. Title.

GE195.T39 2008
333.72—dc22

                                2007038387

Contents

Foreword

The subtitle of this book, "How to Build an Earth-Friendly Community" speaks for my neighbor Nancy Taylor's sensible approach to reducing our environmental footprint. The community is the right scale to address these issues. The individual alone is too small and powerless, national government and Fortune 500 corporations too clueless, too powerful—and out of listening range. But a community is small enough to be real and reachable, something we can all as individuals influence and affect.

The tips found in this book go well beyond switching to hybrids or eight-year lightbulbs. It touches on what greener building standards should be for new houses and commercial space but goes refreshingly further. What would a green hospital look like? Or a green school? How does a community insure the health of its water? What's the proper way, at the neighborhood level, to get people to drive less and still get around? How can local community-based farming help us eat better and become healthier as well as help the environment?

This book answers all these questions with clarity, brevity and insight. It's a worthy read that should have a lot of influential people—a lot of neighbors—talking, then acting.

—Yvon Chouinard, Founder and Owner, Patagonia, Inc.

Acknowledgments

Hillary Clinton said "it takes a village to raise a child," and after writing this book, I know it takes a community to write a book. This book is the work and words of many, crafted by me into these pages. I am grateful for all who have fought for the earth, for justice and for peace, as they have been mentors to me on the path.

Gratitude to Gibbs Smith for inviting me to write this book, for his and Suzanne Taylor's advice and encouragement and for Hollie Keith's editorial skills in crafting the manuscript into a book.

I am grateful to Ted Kerasote, author, seasoned writer and friend, for his wise counsel and advice. Thanks to Carol Wauters and Bill Doyle for their tireless editing and reading skills. Thanks to Brot Coburn, Katherine Ives and Dan Glick for their excellent word-smithing. Thank you to Ellen Fales and Heather Overholser for recycling information. Thanks to Amy Brennan McCarthy for help with my manuscript. Thanks to David Swift for the author photograph. To Rich Anderson, my editor at *Planet Jackson Hole*, for five years of great editing. And to Story Clark for your timely advice. Thanks to Hank Phibbs, John Cooke, Charlie Ross, Robert Gordon and Michael Gross of the Authors Guild for legal advice. Thanks to Tim Sandlin for helping me.

Thank you to Keith and Alisan Peters, and their Carbon Neutral Journal; Dale Sharkey, of Cosmic Apple Gardens; DJ Baxter, of the City of Salt Lake; and Lynn deFreitas, of the FRIENDS of the Great Salt Lake, for being so generous with your time for interviews and for tireless dedication to making this earth a better place.

I am grateful to Mary Bryan and Robert Caine of the Kentfield School District, for the tour of Bacich School, and for your knowledge and dedication to children. In teaching about solar energy and global warming, you are training great citizens of the future!

Thanks to George Brelig for the tour of Fossil Ridge High School in Fort Collins, Colorado, and to Kai Ablekis at Boulder Community Hospital Foothill Campus for the tour of your LEED hospital and all of its many benefits.

Gratitude to Brian Gitt and Bruce Mast of Build It Green for great interviews and all that you do in California. You are a model for the rest of the country. Thanks to Kurt Gottfried of UCS for the book, and a thank-you to Paula Baker-LaPorte for advice and helpful books. Thanks to the Denver Botanic Garden for help with a quotation.

Many thanks to all of my Art of Green Living and Building students over the years, for your curiosity, great questions and interest in greening our community. Thanks, too, to the Green Building Action Team for tireless dedication to green building in Teton County.

A deep bow to Tina Welling, Marcia Craighead and John Travis for keeping me on the path and for inspiring me. Thanks to Linda Morse, and the Wilson Ladies, you know who you are, for love, support and laughter when I most need it. Thanks to my sisters, Anne, Lucy and Susan, for your support and tolerance of my opinions!

Gratitude to Devra Davis, Jack Kornfield, Yvon Chouinard, Mayor Rocky Anderson, Bill McKibben, Robert Collier and Dan Chiras for support and encouragement with my writing; I am deeply inspired by all of you.

To my dear daughters, who walk the green path with brilliance, wisdom and perseverance. You will go far and touch many hearts in the process, including your mother's! To my 19-year-old cat, Babe, who sat in my lap for at least 30,000 of these words, a veritable Tabby muse.

Lastly, and most importantly, I am forever grateful to my partner, and love, Bobby, without whom I could not have written or edited this book. Your endless patience, wisdom, kindness, support and finely honed editing skills made this book possible. Thank you.

Introduction

What would you do if you were told your house is on fire? What if you went to the doctor and got a diagnosis that said you were really sick? When our children or loved ones are suffering greatly, we act, we help out, we gather our wits and find a solution.

Remember the emergency-broadcasting network? Well, this is no longer a test; this high-pitched noise is going to go on and on. From Al Gore, Nicholas Stern, the IPCC (Intergovernmental Panel on Climate Change) and many other organizations that want you to listen. But unlike the stock report or the hog futures or the weather report, the global warming report has deadly consequences.

There is a chart in all of the climate change books and Power Point presentations that shows what will happen if we carry on with business as usual. Driving our cars, shipping our food from a great distance, heating inefficient buildings; all of these actions have costs. Perhaps it is hard for us to relate to a chart. In the movie *An Inconvenient Truth*, there is Al Gore, up on the stage, having to climb a ladder because our carbon emissions are going off the charts!

When I get dire news, I panic. I start spinning my wheels. I get impulsive. During the Loma Prieta earthquake, I grabbed one of my daughter's hands and ran through rippling brick stairs outside. Panic doesn't help anyone, nor does complacency.

There must be a middle way. We each have to find it for our families and ourselves.

Denial won't work, and business will not be usual if we are under water or in the middle of a drought or forest fire.

What are we willing to change? During World War II, people went through deprivation and didn't indulge in the luxuries they were used to like butter and gasoline. Precious commodities were rationed with coupons. We don't like deprivation. There must be a middle ground between denial and deprivation.

This book offers you ways to change your lifestyle, your neighborhood and your practices.

Practices are what they are. Few of us are good at farming all of our own food, and not many of us live off the grid, generating all of our own energy from the sun or wind. But each of us has the ability to be creative. All of us have a caring heart inside, and that capacity must be expanded now.

There is no one way to solve the global warming crisis. Just as it will take many kinds of fuel to replace our appetite for fossil fuel, it will take many different approaches to reduce our carbon footprint. There are actions we can do at home and at work, easy things like changing our lightbulbs, recycling and driving less. There are solutions at the community level, such as starting a Community

Supported Agriculture (CSA) farm or a farmers market or a recycling center. And there are municipal, state and governmental programs we can start in our hometowns. A few ideas are getting your mayor to sign the Climate Protection Agreement, starting a light rail program in your city, redirecting a highway project so it does not damage a fragile ecosystem and making sure there is funding for affordable green housing.

Be creative, do not waste time, get involved with your neighbors—become part of the sustainable earth family. It will change your life!

Save Energy, Save Money

"The human heart and the environment are inseparably linked together. If you think only of yourself, ultimately you will lose."[1]

—the Dalai Lama

We have to stop global warming, and there are a few easy things we can do at home to reduce the amount of energy used. The great news is that each change we make will save us money in the long run. The more efficient our home or apartment, the more money we will have available to pay our rent or mortgage, to buy healthy food for our children or to save for a hybrid car.

Buildings use too much energy. In fact, 76 percent of all power plant–generated electricity is used just to operate buildings.[2] Our homes produce twice the amount of greenhouse gases that our cars do. That means almost every time we use electricity in our homes—for our water heaters, lights or heating—a power plant somewhere is burning coal or natural gas to meet our needs. As a power plant works to produce the electricity that is sent through transmission lines into our homes, it produces carbon dioxide (CO_2) as a waste product. Carbon dioxide is a greenhouse gas and is one of the major culprits creating global warming. In order to reduce the amount of greenhouse gases we produce, we need to find ways to build and live that decrease carbon dioxide in the atmosphere.

How can we do this? We can start by thinking about the ways we use energy in our homes every day.

There are three big energy users in the home: space heating, water heating and lighting. The average homeowner has an energy bill of $1,500 a year. Whether you heat or cool with natural gas, propane, heating oil, electricity or any combination of fuels, all of these sources of fuel produce carbon dioxide. If you have an oil or gas furnace, it releases CO_2 into the air directly at your house. When you use electricity, CO_2 is produced at the coal or gas plant before the energy enters the transmission line to your house. Along the way, the electricity loses power, which makes electric heating and cooling even less efficient and more expensive.

When we cool our homes we are primarily using electricity to run our air conditioners. That, too, leads to global warming. How ironic is it that in an effort to cool our homes, we are making the earth warmer?

There are several practical things you can do to reduce the energy that it takes to heat, light and cool your home.

Energy Audit

• • • • •

Have an energy audit done of your home or apartment. Many utility companies offer programs that, for a small fee, will tell you where the energy leaks are in your home or apartment. If your utility company does not offer an audit, look in the yellow pages for words like "house doctor" or "blower door test." If you institute the recommended changes, you will save a significant amount of energy and money. Some utilities will even rebate their fee and help defray some of your cost. The audit may suggest that you get new energy efficient windows; that you increase the amount of insulation in your walls, ceiling, attic or floor; or that you caulk and weather strip leaks around windows or doors. We lose a third of the heat in our homes through windows and doors. You would be amazed at the amount of energy you can save by making a few select upgrades to your home. Paul Scheckel, author of *The Home Energy Diet*, says, "Energy efficiency is an investment, not a hardship. The cheapest kilowatt is one you don't have to buy—a concept called *negawatts*."[3] I will discuss the easiest changes first, beginning with lighting, then space heating and, lastly, hot water heating.

Lighting
• • • • •

CFLs

The easiest way to create negawatts, watts that you do not use, is to change your lightbulbs from incandescent bulbs to compact fluorescent lightbulbs (CFLs). Each incandescent bulb produces 10 percent light and 90 percent heat. That is not a very efficient way to light or heat our homes! Incandescent bulbs last for about 1,000 hours. CFLs are 75 percent more efficient, last from ten to thirteen years, for 10,000 hours, and pay for themselves very quickly in energy savings. One eighteen-watt CFL will save you $45 over its lifetime alone. Switching out one incandescent lightbulb for one CFL will keep over half a ton of CO_2 out of the atmosphere over the bulb's lifetime. If everyone in the United States switched to CFLs, we could retire ninety power plants from production.

Some people do not want to use CFLs in their homes because they have bad memories of the old fluorescent lights used in schools and offices. New bulbs come in all shapes and sizes, even ones in the shape of a regular lightbulb. They also come in all different color spectra; some give off a warm light similar to the old incandescents.

If everyone in the United States switched to CFLs, we could retire 90 power plants from production.

Others complain that they cannot change to CFLs because their switches are on dimmers. You cannot put a regular CFL in a socket that has a dimmer switch. For these sockets or fixtures you must use a dimmable CFL, and the technology is still in its infancy. My advice would be to try out one dimmable CFL and see how it works and how you like it. The technology is improving as I write. The one drawback of CFLs is that they contain a small amount of mercury, the size of a pinhead, and should not be disposed of in your regular trash. Contact the store where you purchased the bulbs to see if they have a recycling program for your burned-out CFLs. Of course, you may not remember where you got them ten years ago! If you break a CFL, do not inhale or vacuum the mercury; put on rubber gloves, pick it up with a damp cloth and seal the broken bulb and cloth in a plastic bag. Take the contents of the bag to your recycling center on the hazardous waste collection day.

LEDs

Light-emitting diodes (LEDs) could be the light of the future. LEDs use less energy than either incandescents or CFLs, and they last longer. LEDs are made from semiconductors and have been used in commercial applications for years. Many municipalities have converted their signal lights to LEDs and saved thousands of dollars. LEDs are used for architectural lighting, for holiday lights, rope lights, signs and lighting in machines and automobiles. As this book goes to print, LEDs are not quite ready for your reading lamp at home. The cost of production needs to decrease before they will become mainstream, but stay tuned as the technology is improving.

Space Heating
● ● ● ● ●

Space heating uses the most energy in a home. If you live in a cold climate, two-thirds of your energy goes to heating your home. The bigger your home, the more it will cost to heat. If you know your home is an energy sieve, then you know you are essentially heating the neighborhood with your furnace or radiator. If you have insulated your home, have efficient windows and you've caulked your leaks to the outside, you will see a reduction in your heating bill. If you have a furnace, be sure to clean and change the filters. Have an annual inspection to be sure it is working in the most efficient way. Installing a programmable thermostat can save you $150 a year, especially if you work away from home. If you use plug-in electric heaters or portable heaters that look like radiators on wheels, be advised that they cost the same to operate as an electric baseboard. Use them for quick supplemental heat, but not as a primary heat source for a room. The energy costs to run a portable heater will far outweigh the purchase cost very soon after you've bought it. If you have electric baseboard heat, think of switching to another heat source that would be more cost effective such as installing a wood-stove with a catalytic converter. If you live in an apartment, talk to your landlord about an energy audit and see if you can share the costs of upgrading, especially if you are the one paying the utility bills.

Use the sun as much as you can to heat your home; it is free, renewable and does not create CO_2 in our atmosphere. Heating with wood can be a good supplement depending on where you live. The Environmental Protection Agency (EPA) has upgraded the standards for woodstoves to ensure that they put very little particulate matter into the air. Woodstoves with catalytic converters will combust the leftover gases from your wood fire, will burn longer and produce more even heat. Pellet stoves, gas stoves and fireplace inserts all can provide supplemental heat to your living space. Cutting your own wood from a forest of standing dead timber near your home can provide you with a cost-effective fuel that will not put much CO_2 into the atmosphere. On the other hand, open fireplaces, although romantic and beautiful, produce very little heat, sending most of it up the chimney.

Hot Water Heaters
• • • • •

Heating hot water for showers, washing machines and dishwashers is the second-largest consumer of power after space heating. The two main types of water heaters are electric and gas. Electric water heaters tend to use the most power, but they may be the only option in your neighborhood if you do not have natural gas or propane. If you have an electric hot water heater, turn the thermostat down to 120 degrees and put an insulating blanket on the tank to hold in the heat. If your water heater is gas, be sure it is vented to the outside, and get the help of a plumber to add an insulating blanket. It is just a bit more complex than insulating an electric water heater. You do not want to block the vents or flue. If you need to install a water heater, think about using a tankless one. It will cost more up front, but it will save you money and fuel in the long run. Tankless water heaters only heat water on demand. Your conventional water heater keeps heating a large tank full of hot water whether or not there is an immediate need.

Green Tags
● ● ● ● ●

You may have heard of TerraPass or Native Energy or already calculated your carbon footprint on a Web site. Our carbon footprint is calculated based on the amount of energy we use in a year or on a particular trip. In order to figure out how much carbon you are responsible for, you will need your yearly energy use or average monthly utility bill, how many miles you drive in a year and how many airplane trips you take. Each Web site is a little different in helping you make your calculations. In the end, you learn how much carbon your activities produce, and you can purchase green tags to offset your emissions.

You can also buy green tags to offset an individual trip. Many businesses offset all the travel of their employees. If this is not a practice in your office, start your own program.

Green tags should be purchased after you have tried all the conservation measures mentioned above. They are not meant to be a way to carry on our business as usual and then purchase our way out of global warming.

When you purchase green tags, the money you spend funds renewable energy programs.

You may be funding a wind farm in Vermont or a methane generator in Iowa or a solar program in Washington State. Each program is different. Green tags are a way for us to support renewable energy programs and reduce our carbon footprint after conserving.

My daughter got married last summer, and instead of buying each wedding guest a party favor, we bought green tags to offset some of their carbon footprint in getting to the wedding. Very few people flew, most drove, so we estimated the carbon used and purchased green tags on behalf of the wedding guests. We printed out cards left at each guest's place, telling them what a carbon offset is and how they could purchase green tags in the future. Check the resource section at the back of this book for green tag programs.

Case Study

Keith and Alisan saw the film *An Inconvenient Truth* by Al Gore, and it made an impression. But they thought, "We only have one car, we ride our bikes a lot, we have recycled for thirty years, what more can we do?"

Keith offered to help a friend running for office who used the term *carbon neutral* quite often during his campaign. His friend won the election and he and Keith began brainstorming what it really means to be carbon neutral. In the midst of the process, Keith had an epiphany. Waking up in the middle of the night, a voice inside him said, "I've got to do something." He could not go back to sleep and decided he would launch a blog. He envisioned a journal, documenting all the changes he and Alisan would make to reduce their energy use until they were carbon neutral. His blog is called the Carbon Neutral Journal. Starting January 1, 2007, every day for a year, he documents various aspects of going carbon neutral. The blog features something different each day, including choices, tips, rants, opinions and statistics.

The process of going carbon neutral has been methodical for them. Beginning with an energy audit, they changed twenty-three lightbulbs to CFLs, turned down their water heater to 120 degrees, put weather stripping on the front door and turned down the electric baseboard heat. They also plugged every possible gadget and appliance into power strips, which get turned off at night. Power strips save energy by eliminating the electricity used by TVs and computers that draw energy even when turned off. This is true for most digital devices with a plug.

Some strange things happened with their heating bills. The first four months of winter were very cold and their electric bill went up instead of down, but their gas bill for their gas stove upstairs went down. In the end, over a period of eight months, their electric bill was down 10 percent.

Those are the facts, but the greatest aspect of the changes this couple has made is the subtle philosophical shifts. They have gone from being consumers to deciding they can live without the latest and greatest. There is more consideration and deliberation, asking themselves if they really need something before purchasing it. They have cut out extra trips that might not have been given a second thought before. And planning further ahead has helped Alisan save time and energy on her trips. Alisan flies and Keith does not, so she plans ahead, finding bus routes and offsetting the carbon footprint of her trip.

I asked Keith and Alisan about food choices, and it seems they are being more conscious of how far their food has traveled. For example, in the winter they eat fewer bananas since they are shipped from distances, such as Ecuador. Shopping at the farmers market is a favorite pastime and eating as much local food as possible is also important for these two.

(Continued . . .)

I asked what the future holds for them, and both Keith and Alisan dream about their own green home. Right now, being part of a homeowners' association in their area is frustrating. If a homeowner wanted to put solar panels on their roof, it would have to meet the approval of 70 percent of the residents in their community; even clotheslines are outlawed. Once their car dies, they hope there will be a hybrid, biodiesel vehicle that will get great mileage and fit their bikes inside.

This couple is clearly reducing their carbon footprint, having fun doing it and teaching others how to do the same through a daily blog. Visit Keith's blog at www.carbonneutraljournal.com.

Action Points

• • • • •

➲ Go to your local hardware store or lighting center and get help selecting your CFLs. They come in all shapes and sizes and light spectra. Your supermarket may sell CFLs, but if you don't know what you are looking for, it can be confusing. Keep your eyes open for free distribution of CFLs at energy fairs or conferences. Also check for CFL rebates with your local utility company.

➲ Switch every non-dimmable light fixture in your home and office immediately to CFLs.

➲ Put an insulating blanket found at hardware stores on your electric water heater.

➲ Install a programmable thermostat for your heating source.

➲ Call your local utility company and order an energy audit for your home, office or apartment. Institute as many of the audit's suggestions as you can. Check into rebates available from your utility company. Remember that money up front is money saved in the future.

- ➲ Check into federal and state tax incentives and credits for improving your energy efficiency. The current federal tax credit offers up to $2,000 for adding qualified solar water heating and photovoltaic systems to your home. This credit currently expires in December 2008.

- ➲ If you need to take out a home-equity loan to remodel or renovate, try to find a lender that will reduce your payments because you are going green.

- ➲ When a home appliance breaks, be sure to replace it with an Energy Star appliance. Whenever you purchase a computer, TV, DVD player or new phone, make sure it is Energy Star approved.

- ➲ Get power strips for all of your plug-in appliances like phone chargers, stereos, DVDs, TVs and computers. Plug everything with a black transformer box or digital readout into a strip, and then turn the whole strip off at night. This saves you energy.

- ➲ If you are buying or building a new home, apartment or condo, be sure to go green. Ask if green features are incorporated into the building design.

- ➲ Put your outdoor lights on a motion sensor so they work only when you need them and will not be on all night. Use solar outdoor lights; let the sun light your path in the dark.

CHAPTER 2

Remodel Green:
Here Comes the Sun

"The decision to base our heating and energy technology on the power of the sun is not open to sensible debate. There simply is no other long-term solution . . . We have to finally and permanently admit the simple beauty of our situation: It's all about the sun."

—Clarke Snell, Tim Callahan, *Building Green*

The energy crisis of the 1970s sent many of us scrambling to find a better way to inhabit the earth. It was clear we were living beyond our means in terms of fossil fuels. We were on a collision course and something had to be done.

Solar energy represented one option. Using the sun for energy is an ancient concept practiced by many different civilizations. The Anasazi and pueblo peoples in the Four Corners area of Colorado, New Mexico, Arizona and Utah did so many centuries ago. It simply

12

made sense for these ancient peoples to capture the heat of the sun, which fell onto the stones and cliffs that made up their dwellings. The cliff dwellings were warmed by the sun during the day. At night, the absorbed warmth in the stones would radiate into the living space. The back of the dwellings was protected by the thickness of the cliff walls, which provided an insulative barrier.

Passive Solar Design
● ● ● ● ●

When the price of oil began to skyrocket in the 1970s, architects, builders and homeowners turned toward the sun and found that passive solar design offered a great way to save energy. In the winter, when the angle of the sun is low, any south-facing structure will experience solar gain, and its occupants will be warmed through available windows. However, the space will only store and take full advantage of the sun if there is sufficient mass inside the building to absorb the heat. In other words, there must be some kind of heat-absorbing material in your home to soak up the heat from the sun that has come through your windows. Then, when night falls, the solar gain from heat stored in the walls, tiles or concrete slab will provide warmth. I have a four-inch concrete slab floor in my home. Others use concrete walls, bricks or tiles for mass. The important design calculation to make is the ratio of mass to glass. The most common mistake made in passive solar construction is building with too much glass and not enough mass. The prescribed calculation is six to nine times mass to glass. I once made the mistake of building with too much glass and found myself opening windows in January to let out excess heat. This is not a very energy efficient way to live.

In the summer, when the sun was high in the sky, the cliff dwellings did not overheat. The overhang of the cliffs above provided shade from the heat of the sun. Passive solar design made note of this and specifies that you calculate the size of your roof overhang based on the latitude at which you live. This is an easy calculation to make, and you can find the charts in any passive solar handbook. In summer, the overhang shades the glass windows, there is less solar gain and occupants are cool inside the house.

Passive solar design caught on in the 1970s but never reached the mainstream, partly due to the withdrawal of government funding. The Solar Energy Research Institute opened in 1977 in Golden, Colorado, and was funded by the federal government. New books were written and businesses were established to teach us how to orient buildings to the south and capture the light and heat of the sun. This was an exciting time. However, administrations changed and government funding for solar research was substantially reduced. The lack of political backing had an impact on research, government subsidies, tax cuts and other incentives that could have driven the energy efficiency movement forward during the last twenty-five years. Jimmy Carter put solar panels on the White House; Ronald Reagan took them off.

For the next twenty-five years, the solar movement was continued in a small way by dedicated architects, designers, builders and homeowners. This required perseverance and bucking the tide of gross consumerism. The dominant perception that our resources were once again infinite had returned in full force. After the Arab oil embargo was over, the price of oil fell precipitously and ignorance, again, became bliss.

The Green Building Movement
• • • • •

During the 1980s and '90s, scientists began to publish their research on global warming. Shocking data were coming in from the Arctic and Antarctic, indicating that the ice caps were beginning to melt at a more rapid pace. Ice core data was showing an alarming rate of carbon dioxide accumulation in the atmosphere. Still, it was very hard to get government and industry to pay attention to these early clarion calls.

By the 1990s, the building industry began to realize that they were responsible for 48 percent of all greenhouse gas emissions and that 76 percent of all electricity generated by U.S. power plants goes to the building sector.[1] They also began to realize that people were becoming sick as a result of living and working around toxic building materials. In response to these factors, the United States Green Building Council was founded in 1993, to begin to address the use of scarce resources, through energy efficient building materials. It also recognized the health of people who live, work and play in buildings and the effects of toxicity from building materials.

Indoor Air Quality
• • • • •

Since most people spend 90 percent of their time indoors, the air that we breathe inside is very important. Indoor air quality is affected by many sources of indoor air pollution, such as paints, adhesives, finishes and stains, not just dust. Ironically, in 1987, the EPA put new carpet in their building in Washington, D.C., and immediately started receiving complaints from employees in the building. Workers complained of memory loss, migraines, rashes, asthma, chronic fatigue and multiple chemical sensitivities. "The EPA's director of Health and Safety told the *Washington Times* that the 'freshly manufactured carpet clearly caused the initial illness.' Within a few weeks . . . he was removed from his job."[2] The EPA was afraid that it would endanger a billion-dollar carpet industry. The truth is that toxic binders have been used to connect the fabric of a carpet to the backing of a carpet since World War II. Some of the ingredients in carpeting actually include suspected carcinogens, such as formaldehyde, toluene and xylene.

Toxic binders have been used to connect the fabric of a carpet to the backing of a carpet since World War II. Some of the ingredients in carpeting actually include suspected carcinogens, such as formaldehyde, toluene and xylene.

As a green building consultant, I get phone calls from people who are allergic to their homes. The first thing I tell them to check is the carpet. Where did it come from? How new is it and what are the carpet's ingredients? Toxic carpet is a very inexpensive way to cover a floor, but that does not take into account the expense of treating the inhabitants, pets and babies who breathe the "new carpet" smell in a tightly enclosed space. The health costs of treating a child with asthma far outweigh the savings from an inexpensive carpet purchase. Nontoxic carpets are widely available today. They may cost you a little more up front, but you will save in the long run because no one will get sick living with a healthy carpet. You can find healthy carpet sources in the resource section under Carpets and Rugs.

Other culprits that can affect your indoor air quality are paints, stains, adhesives and finishes. All of these products can give off volatile organic compounds (VOCs). VOC is actually a designation used for chemicals that cause smog. If a product gives off fumes that may cause smog, the product must list the amount of VOCs that it contains.

Actually, there are many toxic products in paints and stains that do not cause smog, but they certainly can cause allergic reactions for you and your children. Check the ingredients of any product that you bring into your home. Ask the hardware or paint store for a material safety data sheet (MSDS), which is required by law to tell you what the product contains, unless, of course, it is a trade secret, and then they do not have to reveal that to you. If you are considering using a paint or stain, ask for a small sample, brush it onto a piece of wood or Sheetrock, put it next to your bed, or your child's, for a night, and see if the product causes any reaction, allergy or headache. This is much better than painting the whole room, only to find out you or someone in your family is allergic to the product.

The Precautionary Principle
● ● ● ● ●

At the present time in the United States, it must be proven by scientific study that a chemical causes either cancer or death before it is required to be taken off the market. This leaves the burden of proof with the public whose health is being endangered. Meanwhile, the manufacturers can focus on minimizing their costs.

We do not practice the Precautionary Principle in the United States. This concept says that if we suspect something is toxic, it should not be put into a product. The Precautionary Principle states that "when an activity raises threats of harm to human health or the environment, precautionary measures should be taken even if some cause and effect relationships are not fully established scientifically."[3] The European Union has adopted the Precautionary Principle, which puts the burden of proof on the chemical company not to introduce a particular chemical if it is suspected of causing harm to human health or the environment.

We cannot wait for our government to protect us from toxic chemicals. We must do our homework about what chemicals we introduce into our homes. Do not buy a home with vinyl flooring, windows or walls, if you have any sensitivities or allergies. When vinyl is made, it produces dioxin, which is one of the most toxic substances known to man. Vinyl can continue to off-gas once it is in your home. Pay attention to furniture and carpet treated with anti-stain formulas. Also, beware of permanent press sheets and wrinkle-free clothing, both of which are treated with formaldehyde woven into the fabric to prevent wrinkling. Mattresses, including crib mattresses, are treated with polybrominated diphenylether (PBDE) as a flame retardant, which is a known endocrine disruptor. Some suspect it is related to sudden infant death syndrome. You can find nontoxic bedding in the resource section under Beds, Bedding and Mattresses.

Remodeling Green
• • • • •

If you live in a home or apartment that you want to remodel, then remodel green as much as possible. The goals of a green remodel should be to create a healthier living space that is more energy efficient than your existing space and that is lit with daylight. Finding ways to conserve energy should be the first priority of your remodel. It may seem like a lot of work to remodel your existing living space rather than building a new house, but in the end it will save you money, be less damaging to the environment, use less energy and fewer new materials, and you will not be disturbing a pristine piece of land.

The first thing you need to do is plan ahead. What is your budget? How much will you do yourself, and how much will you hire out to a contractor? Are you going to use an architect? If so, find out if the architectural firm has "green" experience and if it is committed to the basic principles of green design. Has it designed green remodels before? Is it conversant with the materials you plan to use? Call former clients of the architects you are interviewing and ask if their project was finished on time and on budget. Ask if the clients' energy bills are actually lower after the remodel.

Doing a green remodel will require more of your time and ideas than simply turning over your project to an architect. Plan just how you want your space to be, what materials to use, how much sunlight there will be. The "feel" of the room is something only you can know. It is fun to involve yourself with the project. You should have the builder attend the planning meetings, and if you are doing extensive landscaping, involve the landscaper too. You will save money by taking the time to plan extensively on paper before you do something expensively, such as tearing down a wall you later wish you had kept.

When you first meet with your architect or contractor, think about what materials you can salvage from your demolition. In an older building, wood timbers may be hidden by plaster or Sheetrock. Wood or concrete floors can be reused or exposed from under carpets and refinished. Old single-pane windows can be used to divide interior spaces. Be creative; it will save you money not to buy new materials. Don't forget to recycle your construction waste.

Unless your home was built recently, you should consider adding to your insulation because about "65 percent of U.S. houses are poorly insulated, a 2005 Harvard study estimates."[4] After insulation, consider window retrofits and the efficiency of your lighting fixtures and appliances. When you have addressed ways that your existing structure can conserve energy, then you can have the fun of finding ways to use renewable energy to meet your heating and cooling needs.

Insulation

• • • • •

Re-insulating your home or apartment will save you more money than you realize. Check your existing insulation, measure its R-value (resistance to escaping heat) and see where you can easily add more insulation. These topics should all be covered in an energy audit. If you are going to re-roof, be sure to add insulation to the roof and attic. Adding rigid foam board to your existing roof may be the most cost-effective and energy efficient way to go. For your attic, you can blow in cellulose or foam or use batts of recycled cotton. Insulating your attic will hold in the winter heat and keep out the summer heat. Don't forget corners that tend to leak air in or out.

For your living areas, there are many different ways to retrofit your insulation, but you want to be sure you are not using toxic insulation. If you go with sprayed foam, be sure it is formaldehyde-free, water-based as opposed to petroleum based, and that it finishes off-gassing within a few hours. Also be sure that you, your family and pets are not around when the foam is being sprayed. Give the insulation plenty of time to finish off-gassing and airing out before you return. If you use fiberglass, use a brand that does not contain formaldehyde and that contains recycled glass content. If you don't like fiberglass, use a recycled blue jean batt product called Ultratouch. You can blow in cellulose, which is made of old newspapers, but you want to be sure you are not allergic to the off-gassing of the old printing ink. It is time for you to do your homework. Ask questions that will assure your indoor air quality will not be compromised by your new insulation.

If you are going to re-roof, be sure to add insulation to the roof and attic. Adding rigid foam board to your existing roof may be the most cost-effective and energy efficient way to go.

Insulation not only holds in your heat, it keeps your house measurably cooler in the summer too. With summer temperatures climbing higher and higher, your insulation could save you significant money in cooling costs as well. If you have done an energy audit, you may be able to get some financial help from your utility company for re-insulating. Check recent federal and state tax laws, which should give tax credits for insulating.

Windows
● ● ● ● ●

After you have thought about insulation, what about your windows? Are they old single-pane windows? Are they perfectly good double-pane windows but mostly on the north side of your living space? Adding windows on the south-facing side of your home or apartment will increase your daylight, will warm your living space and will save you energy. Remember to put some mass into the space so you truly have a passive solar room and not a hot house. The strategy for passive solar heating is relatively simple, but it must be done right from the start. There must be more square footage of mass—a heat-absorbent material like concrete or brick—than the square footage of glass. If you cannot pour a concrete slab or floor, think of using sand as a bed for recycled tiles or bricks that are dark in color, to absorb the solar heat coming through your windows.

Windows come in many different materials. Try to install wood windows, or at least ones that have wood on the inside and metal on the outside. Several manufacturers of wood windows are making windows with Forest Stewardship Council (FSC) wood. That means that the wood has been sustainably harvested and that their logging practices are fair to the employees and kind to the environment. Fiberglass windows are okay but cannot be recycled, aluminum windows are not very efficient and vinyl windows should not be installed because they are simply not a green product. Windows have different ratings depending on the coating, gas between the panes and how much heat they keep in or out. If you are going to use your windows for passive solar heating on the south side of your home or in a sunny space, be sure your windows allow some heat and sun to come into the space. I have seen sunrooms that are constantly chilly because the windows are too efficient at keeping the sun and heat out. Plan for some kind of window quilt or heavy curtain to hold in your heat at night. Even the best windows loose heat at night when the temperature outside drops below the temperature inside.

After you have thought about insulation and about your windows, see what other energy-saving strategies you can implement.

Appliances
• • • • •

Anytime you buy an appliance, be sure that it is an Energy Star appliance. The Energy Star program is sponsored by the EPA in

partnership with the Department of Energy. The Energy Star pr
has ratings for everything from battery chargers to traffic lights.
can even build your home according to Energy Star guidelines. David
Johnston and Kim Master say in their book, *Green Remodeling*, that
"Energy Star appliances can save the typical U.S. household about 30
percent of its appliance energy bills. . . . Over the next 15 years, full
adoption of Energy Star appliances could save American households
as much as $100 billion."[5]

Water Heaters
• • • • •

Hot water heaters are responsible for about 20 percent of the energy
used in a home. Most water heaters with a tank need replacement
after about ten years. If your hot water heater is ready to be replaced,
think about replacing it with a tankless water heater. Tankless heaters
have been used extensively for many years in Japan and Europe, where
energy costs more and space may be at a premium. A tankless heater
could save you 15 to 20 percent on your utility costs because it does
not have to keep your water hot all the time, causing what is called a
"standby loss" of heat.[6]

Tankless hot water heaters are made in both electric and gas
models. Electric tankless water heaters cost less to purchase, but you
must consider operating costs that may be excessive. If your house is
small and there are not long runs of plumbing between demand sites
such as shower, clothes washer and dishwasher, then electric may be
the way for you to go. If you buy a gas tankless water heater, the purchase price will be more than an electric heater, and you will have to
locate it where it can be vented outside. The cost of natural gas or
propane may save you more than heating your water with electricity.

As you can see, there are many variables involved in switching from a tank water heater to a tankless, but as energy costs rise, tankless will be the way to go. Be sure to check both the purchase price and the operating costs over the life of the appliance. Don't trust an initial low purchase price only to find out it costs you a small fortune in energy bills. It is best to check with your utility company, gas supplier, landlord and plumber to see what the most cost-effective choice is for you in your location.

Hot water heaters are responsible for about 20 percent of the energy used in a home.

As saving energy becomes more and more important, wasting energy by keeping water hot in a tank for twenty-four hours a day just does not make sense.

Washing Machines

The old top-loading washing machines use a great deal of water and energy. Front-loading washing machines use 40 to 60 percent less water and 30 to 50 percent less energy.[7] You could save as much as 30 to 50 percent on your energy bill by replacing a top-loading machine with a front-loading one.

Why are front-loading washing machines better? They operate in a different way; instead of agitating the clothes in the old-fashioned way, front loaders slowly turn the clothes on a horizontal axis and then stop to cover all the clothes with water and soap. Front loaders use less energy to run, they create less damage to your clothes, they use less soap and, at the end, they spin your clothes so fast they are almost dry. If you wash your clothes using cold water, you will also save 90 percent of the energy that goes just to heat the water to wash your clothes. Instead of using a dryer, put your clothes on a rack and dry them in a south window, or when weather permits, hang your clothes outside on a clothesline. Some subdivisions have ordinances about not using clotheslines because they are unsightly! Try to get these regulations changed. How will we ever save energy with laws like these?

Refrigerators

We've come a long way from the icebox, particularly since the government set new energy efficient standards for refrigerators in 2001. "A typical new refrigerator with automatic defrost and a top-mounted freezer uses less than 500 kWh [kilowatt hours of electricity] per year, whereas a typical model sold in 1973 used over 1,800 kWh per year."[8]

When you are purchasing a new refrigerator, carefully estimate your needs and choose the most energy efficient one in the size you need. It is better to purchase a more spacious refrigerator than to keep a separate fridge in the garage or basement just to keep beverages cool.

The side-by-side refrigerators as well as the ones with a built-in water and ice dispenser in the door will cost you more in dollars and energy. It is easy enough to make ice inside the freezer.

Dishwashers

If you are replacing or installing a new dishwasher, be sure it is Energy Star rated to be a low-water-use washer with the ability to turn off the drying cycle. Only run the dishwasher when it is full, and turn your hot water heater thermostat down to 120 degrees. Let the dishwasher coil heat the water to a sterilizing temperature. Researchers have done tests to see if you use more water washing dishes by hand or by machine. The new low-water machines won because they use less water than running the water over the dishes and rinsing them by hand. It takes roughly twenty-five gallons to wash dishes by hand, and six gallons to wash dishes in a water-wise dishwasher.[9] David Johnston and Kim Masters say "an Energy Star qualified dishwasher can save you more than $30 a year in energy costs."[10]

Greening your Office
• • • • •

Many of the points made above could apply to renovating your office, business or factory. To green your office from the inside, follow these action points.

Action Points
• • • • •

⊃ Start an office recycling program, especially for paper and ink cartridges.

⊃ Install a programmable thermostat, and heat the office only when occupied.

⊃ Buy only Energy Star computers, monitors, faxes and copiers.

⊃ Plug all machines into power strips and turn them off when you leave the office.

⊃ Set computer monitors to sleep or turn off after a few minutes.

⊃ Install motion sensors for lights, so offices and bathrooms are lit only when occupied.

⊃ Do a lighting audit; change out old fluorescents for T-8 lighting. T-8s are long fluorescent tubes that are used in office settings; they are for commercial spaces. Switching from old T-12 tubes to

T-8s can save your business as much as 30 percent in energy costs. Some utility companies will contribute to a commercial lighting retrofit. The CFLs for residential use are curly and fit in a regular lamp. T-8s are long tubes that fit in commercial fixtures. They replace the less efficient long tubes and ballasts and therefore save a business money.

- Join a purchasing group for paper, food items and bulk equipment. Check the resource section under Office/Home Office for suggestions.

- Create a scrap paper box for notes and phone messages.

- Buy only recycled paper products, printer paper, toilet paper and paper towels.

- If your business prints pamphlets or literature, use recycled paper and vegetable inks.

- Recycle or refill ink cartridges.

- Print double sided, which saves paper and money.

- When printing, use the "draft" option to save ink until your final document.

- Educate your employees about your new recycling and energy efficient programs.

- After several programs are in place, publicize your green programs to your customers. It can help you to "grow" your business.

CHAPTER 3

Green Building

"Nature—with its complex, local ecological systems and myriad life forms—cannot speak at our construction sites. The mahogany tree and black leopard have no voice in our government chambers, corporate boardrooms, or local wood shops. It is our responsibility to speak on their behalf as best we can. . . . There is still time to change paths and stabilize what remains of natural forests, while providing for society's construction needs."[1]

—*Building With Vision*

The green building industry is booming. In fact, as other sectors of the construction industry languish, green building is going strong. The boom has been encouraged by people's awareness of indoor air quality, the potential for energy savings and a heightened sense of each individual's contribution of carbon dioxide to the atmosphere. There is also increased availability of very attractive, durable green building and furnishing materials.

Various incentives for building green are offered by municipalities. See if your town or county will help you go green. Some cities and counties will fast track your building permit, waive your permit fee or offer a refund for the building fee upon completion of the building, if it meets green building standards.

For commercial buildings, *USA Today* reports, "the federal government, 15 states and 46 cities require new public buildings to meet the U.S. Green Building Council's LEED standards (Leadership in Energy and Environmental Design), which require non-toxic building materials among other things."[2] The cities of Boston and Washington, D.C., have carried green requirements into the private sector by mandating that any building over 50,000 square feet meet LEED standards. Boston will require that private buildings over 50,000 square feet achieve the LEED Certified level, which is the least stringent of the LEED categories. Washington, D.C., will require all publicly financed buildings over 10,000 square feet to meet LEED requirements by 2008. Washington, D.C., is also looking into requiring all of its schools to be green.

Large-scale developments got a boost from the Green Building Council in January 2007 when it offered to waive the certification fee for buildings that are constructed according to LEED Platinum requirements, the most stringent of LEED standards. The fee will be refunded at the completion of the building. On a large project, the certification fee for Platinum can be thousands of dollars.

Green buildings, whether they are LEED or Energy Star, residential or commercial, are better for the environment by virtue of the materials used in building. Green buildings are also good for their inhabitants because their indoor air quality is much cleaner due to decreased off-gassing from cabinets, flooring and paint. Even though new energy codes require that buildings be tighter; i.e., better insulated with less infiltration of outside air through windows and doors, our buildings must be filled with fresh air to keep the occupants healthy. This seeming paradox can be achieved in most new homes that have air-to-air heat exchangers or a whole-house fan in the attic to exhaust the stale air and bring in new fresh air without making the building cold. Many new office buildings are built with operable windows or with fresh air controls at every workstation.

Green Homes
• • • • •

Before you decide to build a green home from scratch, be sure you have ruled out the option of remodeling your existing home or apartment or buying an existing home and doing a green remodel. Both of the above options could save you significant money, disturb less land and use fewer building materials. That said, if you decide to buy land, it is important to take several things into account:

1. Is the land close to public transportation either by biking or walking?

2. Is the land near utilities; i.e., electricity, phone, high-speed Internet service, etc.? Or are you willing and prepared to live off the grid?

3. Is the land in a community that will be supportive of your kids with good schools within walking or biking distance? Is there potential for organic gardening or a farmers market?

4. Be sure you choose a building site with solar options. The best option for passive solar is to face the house south, with the length of the house located on an east-west axis. If you do not have that option, be sure you have room on a south-facing roof for photovoltaic and solar thermal panels, and that a neighboring house, office building or large tree will not cast a shadow, making it impossible for you to optimize your south-facing solar gain.

5. If you cannot afford to install solar now, be sure you put in plumbing and wiring to accept solar panels later. In the future, solar panels will be more efficient in their vertical format, and you may be able to place solar panels on a vertical wall or on a solar panel tracker near the south side of your house. If this is the case, be sure you know what your neighbor's plans are so they will not block the sun from getting to your panels with future buildings.

Once you have found your building site, make it a priority to find an architect and builder who have both done green projects, then decide what kind of house you need. The average size of houses has grown enormously over the last twenty years. Instead of conserving, we have been getting more wasteful. The average home size in 1950 was 1,000 square feet. In 2004, the average size had more than doubled to 2,340 square feet.[3] At the same time that our houses have gotten larger, our families have gotten smaller, leaving a vast amount of unused space that requires heating, lighting and cooling. Determine how much space you really need. Consult the book *The Not So Big House* by Sarah Susanka, or *The New Ecological Home* by Dan Chiras.

Siting Your House
• • • • •

Plan your building site to create as little disturbance to the land as possible. Take some time to get to know the site; walk on it, picnic on it, camp on it. Spend time on the land in all four seasons of the year since part of building green involves our relationship to nature. Green building is an interactive process, not just plunking down a building on a piece of land as fast as possible. Learn where the prevailing wind comes from and, if you are in a hot climate, how your building site will be shaded.

When I purchased land to build my first solar house, I spent time skiing up to the proposed home site, measuring how the sun hit the land at different times of day. I noted how short the winter days were, and that changed the solar orientation of the house before it was built. Take some time; you will be glad you did. Hopefully your home will be there for a very long time, so it is worth the long planning process. Minimize the number of trees you will have to cut down; do not disturb fragile habitat for plants or animals. Keep drainage and erosion in mind if you build into a hillside. Work with the builder to minimize site damage, saving the topsoil to put back on the land when your house is complete. Mark the building envelope and don't allow heavy equipment to disturb the surrounding land.

Learn where the prevailing wind comes from and, if you are in a hot climate, how your building site will be shaded.

Sometimes you will have to take aggressive action to protect existing trees and fragile habitat. Strong protective fences may need to be raised. Your builder may understand your intentions, but not every backhoe operator or delivery driver may share this belief. There is a way to build with minimum impact, and it may require re-educating your sub-contractors that they are working on land that you care about.

Choosing Building Materials
• • • • •

There are many wonderful options for building green that do not use up precious resources. Right now in the United States, 40 percent of our wood goes into buildings. "It is estimated that an acre of forest— up to 44 trees—goes into the 12,500 board feet that make up the average 2,000-square-foot home in the United States."[4] This is due to the typical wood-frame construction of most U.S. housing. Many green buildings use alternatives to wood framing. Some use wall and roof materials such as Structurally Insulated Panels (SIPs) or Insulated Concrete Forms (ICFs). Others use local materials like mud, straw, clay or earth to form the walls.

Structurally Insulated Panels
• • • • •

A SIP is a structurally insulated panel that looks like a sandwich, also called a Stress Skin Panel. It has a sheet of wood material on either side of a core. The outside of the sandwich is usually made of oriented strand board (OSB), which is made with small chips of wood or some recycled material bonded together to make a sheet of wood. The strand board, which resembles plywood, forms the interior and exterior of the SIP. Sandwiched between the two pieces of board is a core of foam or wheat straw. The core in a SIP provides the insulation value, and the whole panel comes as a complete unit, ready to be installed. Many homes use SIPs on their roofs as well. The walls and roof of a house can be pre-designed with the exact dimensions specified and ordered from a SIP manufacturer. The SIP panels for a whole house can be delivered on a truck, ready to be installed as walls or a roof. SIPs can significantly reduce the amount of time it takes to build your house. Also, SIPs produce very little waste as each panel is pre-designed. The plumbing and wiring can be preplanned so channels are cut in the SIPs ahead of time at the factory. If you are highly allergic, be sure to find SIPs that have wood panels bonded with a nontoxic binder, not formaldehyde. Also be certain the core in the SIP does not aggravate your allergies.

Insulated Concrete Forms
• • • • •

ICFs vary more in form and size than SIPs, and they use concrete to make the inside more stable. Some ICFs are made of recycled materials; some are entirely new; some are a combination. A great feature of ICFs is their insulative value. The walls in my house are made of Perform Wall, a type of ICF, which is 85 percent post-industrial Styrofoam mixed with concrete. The core of each block is hollow in a honeycomb pattern. The inside is made strong by putting rebar (steel reinforcing rod) in the center, and then pouring concrete around it. The walls in my house are fourteen inches thick. The ICF wall is the structure, the insulation and the sound barrier all in one. ICFs do not require any additional insulation, and they can be plastered or Sheetrocked directly on the inside and stuccoed on the outside. Some ICFs are the size of concrete blocks, and others are ten feet long, stacking together like Lego blocks. ICFs can be used for your foundation as well. Once the concrete is poured and the wall is in place, there is no need for forms, bracing or framing lumber.

If you are going to build using an ICF system, be sure to specify that fly ash be used in your concrete. Traditionally, concrete is made up of aggregate (gravel) and portland cement. The trouble with portland cement is that it is very energy intensive to manufacture. In fact, the process of making it is responsible for 6 to 8 percent of carbon dioxide emissions worldwide. Fly ash is a waste product that comes from the smokestacks of coal-fired plants. Most of our electricity comes from the burning of coal. Fly ash can replace portland cement by up to 65 percent in your concrete. Fly ash in your concrete takes longer to cure but makes the concrete more durable. Fly ash also puts a waste product to good use, and it saves the planet from the manufacture of portland cement and its carbon dioxide emissions.

Alternative Natural Materials
• • • • •

People have used natural materials in their buildings for centuries, and many of these building arts have been revived in the last twenty to thirty years. Cob, adobe, rammed earth, straw bale and stone make beautiful natural homes. The natural alternatives for green building often use less transportation energy than SIPs and ICFs. "Before the advent of the hardware superstore with attached cappuccino bar and playground, humans were stuck building houses from materials they could gather themselves."[5]

Straw may not be available in your part of the country, but the soil may be perfect for a cob house. If you live in a place that has good clay, a cob or rammed earth house might be the best design for you. Cob is the material you see in many of the houses in the British Isles, many of them hundreds of years old. The clay is mixed with sand and sometimes straw and can be formed directly into a wall. Cob is beautiful and can be shaped for lovely arched windows and doorways, but it can be lacking in insulative value in a cold climate.

Adobe is similar to cob and has been used for hundreds of years in South America, Mexico and the American Southwest. The clay mixture is shaped into bricks and left to dry before being constructed into a wall.

Another form of building material that uses the earth is called rammed earth construction. Rammed earth is just that—earth mixed with concrete is compacted between two wooden forms, similar to pouring concrete for foundations. As the earth is compacted and dried, it forms a wall that can be the finished product. Depending on your climate, some builders place insulation in the middle or outside of the rammed earth, which increases the capacity of the wall to keep heat out or in.

If you live near a source of straw, then it may make sense for you to build a straw bale house. Straw is the leftover fibrous product after cereal grains have been harvested and is different from hay. It is hollow; hence the name for the drinking straw, and that makes it an excellent insulator. Straw bale houses insulate themselves, using the thickness of the wall to keep heat in during the winter and out in summer. Straw bales can also be used as the infill material in a timber frame house. Some communities located in active seismic zones will not allow straw bales to be used as the structure for a house, but only as an infill material. This means that the framing members or timbers are the structure and the straw bale is the wall material, but it does not support the roof.

Building with Wood

● ● ● ● ●

Wood or stick frame building is still the primary method of building used in the United States. Carpenters are trained to work with wood. Wood is more readily available at your local lumber store than SIPs or ICFs. In some parts of the country, and depending on the design of your building, wood may still be the least expensive way to build. If you choose wood, see if you can find wood that is certified to be less environmentally harmful. There are two main organizations that certify wood, the Forest Stewardship Council and the Sustainable Forest Initiative. As our forests become depleted in the United States and we rely on lumber from abroad, it is important that the wood be certified so the buyer knows it was grown using sustainable practices and that the forest was not heavily sprayed with pesticides and herbicides that could damage watersheds.

Advanced Framing

In addition to using certified wood, try to use advanced framing techniques. Advanced framing, or Optimum Value Engineering (OVE), is a way of minimizing the use of wood and maximizing the use of insulation to make a building with less heat loss. Heat escapes faster and cold enters more quickly through wood than through insulation. If you place the lumber on twenty-four-inch centers, twenty-four inches apart from each other instead of sixteen-inch centers, you leave more room for insulation and less wood for cold entry. If you use two-by-six dimensional lumber instead of two-by-four dimensional lumber, you increase the space for insulation. There are other technical aspects to OVE having to do with the way you frame your corners, windows and roof. Be sure your builder knows about advanced framing and that the engineers have approved it with your building permit.

Ventilation

Because many houses are so well built now, the air inside a house can become very stale, even toxic. It is extremely important that you design some kind of ventilation system that gives you an air exchange on a regular basis. While my house was being built, I was living in a little log cabin that had its own natural ventilation. When it was snowing and the wind was blowing, I would wake up with snow on my pillow! The logs had shrunk and daylight was visible through the cracks. Upon moving into my new green home, which is tightly insulated, I found the air-to-air heat exchanger I had incorporated provided plenty of ventilation. It exchanges the air every twenty minutes. It brings in fresh outside air that passes close by the air leaving the house in an exchanger. This captures the heat from the inside air before it leaves. That way, the fresh cold air is tempered before being blown through my house. It is also filtered.

Embodied Energy

• • • • •

Embodied energy is a concept that you must take into account if you are building a new building or remodeling. It has to do with all the energy it takes to make a particular material, the energy it takes to ship the material, and then where the material goes at the end of its life. Bamboo is a good example of a green building material that is a wonderful renewable resource, but it does have issues of embodied energy. It is a grass that renews itself in four to seven years. However, the cut bamboo is heat treated to form it into flooring and attach it to a backing. That heating process takes energy. Most of the bamboo used for flooring and furniture is grown in China, so it has the added cost of energy used for transportation to get it to your building site. At the end of its life, it can be easily recycled, which is a good thing. Bamboo is starting to be grown and manufactured in the United

States; that will reduce some of the embodied energy and make it a more sustainable product.

The embodied energy in a cob house would be very low, as the materials to build the walls come from the building site itself. There is no shipping, and the material returns to the land in two or three hundred years as a natural product.

This concept of embodied energy should ideally be applied to all materials in your green home.

Action Points

- • • • •

➲ Site your house to take advantage of solar energy, both passive and active.

➲ Be careful with the size of your home. The less space you have to heat and cool, the better for your wallet and the planet.

➲ Insulate with nontoxic insulation, but use plenty of it.

➲ Choose Energy Star appliances and water-saving fixtures.

➲ If you are not installing solar panels when you build, at least plumb and wire for them so they can be added easily in the future.

➲ Don't forget your solar and insulation tax credits from the federal government and possibly your state or county.

➲ Choose your building materials for practicality and the least amount of embodied energy.

➲ If you build with wood, use advanced framing when you can.

➲ Be sure you put in an air-to-air heat exchanger.

➲ If you landscape, use drought-tolerant plants and shade the west side of your home.

In 2002 and 2003, I helped design and build my green home in northwestern Wyoming.

I picked the site because of its great southern exposure, it was flat and it had no trees to be cut down. I wanted to use the sun to heat and light my home as much as possible because Wyoming winters can be long and cold. I learned from building a passive solar house in Montana in the 1980s that when it is twenty degrees below zero, it is usually sunny.

The walls in my new home are made of Perform Wall, which is an ICF. The thick walls provide structure, insulation and sound proofing—all in one. The roof and floors are also insulated with nontoxic foam, and the windows are very energy efficient.

In addition to the house being oriented to the south, I use photovoltaic panels to generate some of my electricity and solar thermal panels to preheat domestic hot water with the sun. As a result, I use about a third of the energy of the conventionally built home in my region. The floors are warmed by radiant in floor heat that uses a propane boiler to preheat the liquid flowing through tubes in my concrete floors. When the propane delivery truck comes by the house to check my tank to see if I need a refill, he shakes his head and turns his truck around because I use less propane than the average house in my neighborhood.

I use CFLs in most of my light fixtures, and power strips to turn off phantom loads of electricity at night. Zones control the radiant heat, so I can leave several rooms unheated in the winter unless I need to use them.

One holiday season, it was thirty degrees below zero for about a week. I was out of town when the igniter on my boiler broke, meaning there was no mechanical heat in the house. The woman feeding my cats noticed that it was getting colder inside the house. It hit fifty degrees, but then it stayed at that temperature for several days with only the passive solar heat gain from the sun. The boiler man knew my house would hold the heat, so he enjoyed his holiday until he had time to fix the igniter.

In the summer, the reverse is true. At night, I open windows, which allows cold air to sink into the concrete floor. During the day with the windows closed, the concrete cools the house. People often ask if I have air conditioning. In a sense I do, but it does not require any electricity.

I cannot say enough about the joys of living in a green home, built with healthy materials and heated by the sun. It is cozy, warm and welcoming on a freezing-cold day, and conversely cool and quiet on a hot summer day. When people walk into my home they say "it feels so good in here." Believe me, it has nothing to do with my interior decorating but rather with the feeling of living with natural materials. All of the paint, stains and finishes are nontoxic, with beeswax finish on the walls, and natural wool carpets. The kitchen floor is cork, which provides a soft surface for standing at the sink, and also for accidentally dropping dishes! The stairs are bamboo, and beetle-killed logs make up the ceiling beams.

CHAPTER 4

Green Schools and Hospitals

"High performance schools provide superior indoor air quality by controlling sources of contaminants and supplying proper ventilation, resulting in fewer student sick days and increased average daily attendance. Since a majority of a school's operating budget is directly dependent on average daily attendance, even a small increase can significantly boost the operating budget."[1]

—The City of Stockton, California

Green Schools

. . . . .

From the time they are four or five, American children spend at least seven hours a day in school. The hours in school add up to more waking hours than they are at home. Yet until recently, few have considered the environmental quality of the school buildings or the quality of the air the students and teachers breathe.

Learning is important. PTAs, school boards and concerned parents have focused on teachers and the curriculum for a long time. Now we are becoming aware that buildings can influence learning too, and that toxins in our air affect the brain.

As a result, schools are being planned and built according to green guidelines. Green schools, also known as sustainable schools or high performance buildings, are becoming the wave of the future. Many cities, states and counties are mandating that all new schools be green.

No wonder. Green schools save the school districts money. A green building may cost more to build because of increased design time, the hiring of consultants and the use of selected building materials. However, once a green school is up and running, the cost savings begin. Typically, heating and cooling costs are reduced from 20 to 40 percent, and water usage is reduced by about 20 percent. And schools built with green materials, and heated and cooled efficiently, will reduce the amount of carbon dioxide put into the atmosphere.

Daylighting

• • • • •

One key feature of new green schools is in their creative use of daylight. Students go to school in the day, so there is no need for them to be in cavernous classrooms without windows, sitting under artificial lights. In a green school, it is possible to work with natural light, which turns out to be better for the student's concentration abilities and overall learning. Test scores in green schools show a 20 percent improvement over students tested in non-green schools. Studies show that the brain works better in a daylit environment. A study conducted by the Heschong Mahone Group, which looked at the test scores of students in over 2,000 classrooms in three school districts, found that "students with the most classroom daylight progressed 20 percent faster in one year on math tests and 26 percent faster on reading tests than those students who learned in environments that received the least amount of natural light."[2] Studies also show that dental cavities are lessened by exposure to Vitamin D. So students in daylit schools may have fewer visits to the dentist. Bones also grow faster and stronger when the skin is exposed to daylight.[3]

Test scores in green schools show a 20 percent improvement over students tested in non-green schools. Studies show that the brain works better in a daylit environment.

Teachers also like working in green schools where the air quality is better and there is increased ventilation, plenty of sunlight and less noise. Green schools have fewer turnovers in staffing; the same is true in green industries. In general, all people like to work in green buildings. Good indoor air quality helps people do their jobs more efficiently, the brain works better and there are fewer sick days and fewer allergies.

Green School Building
• • • • •

The long-term financial benefits of going green far outweigh the increased cost of designing and building a high performance building. Green schools can cost between $1 and $4 more per square foot to build. Some of the increased costs come from the durable building materials themselves. Other costs come from more sophisticated heating and cooling equipment, such as geothermal heat pumps, which are costly to install, but pay for themselves in a matter of years.

The green cost savings usually run $70 per square foot, which is more than ten times the initial expense of going green. Some of these savings are direct energy savings and some are calculated based on benefits like the increased attendance rates due to decreased absenteeism in green schools.

Persuading parents or architects to convince a school board and district office that it will be worth the increased cost to build a green school is a matter of education. Districts just do not normally take into account the dollars that they will save by going green.

School boards need to look at the design process in a new way that is called integrated design. The design team should be composed of an architect, contractor, teacher, student, school board members, representatives from the administrative staff, the maintenance staff and a landscaper. That way, when the building is designed, all players have a say in what will make the most efficient school for their needs. Closets end up in the right places and mechanical systems are designed to work at optimum efficiency. Students and teachers get a say in how they want to see the classrooms designed to meet their needs. The school board knows the costs from the beginning, and the maintenance staff gets to have a say in how they will maintain the building. Since indoor air quality is a key component of a green school, it is important for windows to be operable and the mechanical heating, ventilation, air conditioning (HVAC) system to be easy to operate. If there are motion sensors in each classroom that control the lights, heat and computers, they need to work in a convenient way for the teachers and students. Since daylighting is a key component of green schools, classrooms need to be able to operate without the fluorescent lights on and without the glare of sunlight that overheats the room and makes it hard to read a computer monitor. All of these design aspects can be worked out with the integrated design team so that the school will operate smoothly and efficiently.

Indoor Air Quality
• • • • •

The Global Green Schools Initiative states that "One half of our nation's 115,000 schools have problems linked to indoor air quality."[4] Although many of us are concerned about our children breathing smog or being exposed to environmental pollutants, it has taken a long time to become aware that our indoor air quality may actually be worse than it is outdoors. The EPA warns us that indoor pollutants may be two to five times greater than outdoor pollutants.[5]

Particularly in buildings where the windows do not open, materials like paints, particleboard, adhesives and furniture continue to off-gas long after the school has been built. In addition, children have smaller lungs, smaller livers and less tolerance for processing pollutants than adults. In the United States, many pollutant-tolerance-dose levels are set based on the dosage an adult male can tolerate. Many believe that childhood asthma rates are skyrocketing partly due to the chemical soup that off-gasses into our homes and schools.

There are other costs of hazardous indoor air quality. Across the United States, public schools are given an allowance for Average Daily Attendance (ADA). If a child is absent, the school does not get funding for that child for that day. This has a cumulative financial consequence for a school district that has a large absenteeism rate.

Energy Efficiency
● ● ● ● ●

With the increased public awareness of global warming and of the levels of carbon dioxide emitted by buildings, districts have begun to pay attention to the carbon footprint of new school buildings. This means each new school would be designed to minimize the amount of carbon dioxide it emits into the atmosphere. Many schools in cold climates, such as Colorado and Wyoming, are finding that installing a geothermal or ground source heat pump can save the school district many times over the cost of installation. Carbon emissions from a ground source heat pump are less than emissions from a traditional boiler system that is used for heating and cooling a school. The idea behind a ground source heat pump is that the ground, below frost level, stays at a constant temperature, about fifty-two degrees Fahrenheit. If water is drawn from a well at forty-two degrees and circulated through tubes in the ground, the ground will heat the water ten degrees. Then the fifty-two-degree water is sent to the boiler, and it takes less energy to get it to the right temperature to heat the building. Because the constant ground temperature is heating the fluid that is used for the mechanical system, it is more efficient and less polluting. Some schools have automatic dimmer switches on the fluorescent lights so that as sunlight enters the classroom through the windows, the lights automatically dim, saving energy.

Other energy savers deal with water use. Faucets and toilets can teach kids about saving water. Some schools use waterless urinals and timed faucets, which can reduce the school's water use by up to 20 percent. Schools also can save water by collecting rainwater and reusing it for irrigation and by landscaping with native plants and grasses that require very little water or expensive maintenance.

Case Study One model school in the Kentfield School District of California has zeroed out its power bill by installing photovoltaic panels. The district floated a bond issue in 2004 to support 50 percent of the purchase price of the panels and received a rebate from the Self-Generation Incentive Program of Pacific Gas and Electric for the other 50 percent of the cost. The system generates 240,000 kWh, which is enough to power forty-one homes. The district saves $100,000 on its energy bills and keeps 180 tons of carbon dioxide out of the atmosphere every year.

Renewable energy can be used as an educational tool too. Why not educate our children about the benefits of converting from fossil fuel–based energy to renewable sources? The sixth-grade science classes at the Bacich School in the Kentfield School District study solar energy. They know the amount of solar electricity that their school generates, and they also learn about grid inter-tie. There is an interactive kiosk in the school library that shows how much energy the panels are generating at that moment. If there is more energy being generated than used by the school, it is sold back to the utility. This is called grid inter-tie. As California's energy costs continue to climb, the Kentfield School District is ensuring that they have a guaranteed source of power that is both non-polluting and cost effective. As children learn about the sun as a source of energy, they can carry this knowledge into the workplace and into their future homes.

Involving Youth in Combating Global Warming

The Bacich School District has also initiated a program called "Cancel a Car," which teaches students (and parents) about activities at home that reduce their use of energy. Each student is given a coupon book to take home that encourages activities such as recycling, turning down the thermostat and walking or biking to school. Other coupons include changing from incandescent lightbulbs to CFLs and using reusable containers in their school lunches, such as a thermos instead of a disposable plastic water bottle or box juice. As students complete each of these activities, they fill out a coupon and bring it back to school. A team of volunteers calculates the equivalent amount of energy saved by the children's activities, measures the savings in pounds of carbon dioxide and adds it up.

Each time 12,000 pounds of carbon dioxide has been saved—which is equivalent to taking one car off the streets for a year—they portray this on a banner in front of the school, which shows a car with a red line through it. In six months they cancelled sixty-six cars, or 800,000 pounds per year of carbon dioxide. Cancel a car!

In addition to teaching kids how to save energy at home, this program is a clever way to teach parents to break their energy-intensive habits. It is much easier to support our kids in a school project than it is to think about breaking our dependence on driving to the store rather than walking. When your child reminds you to recycle, you are much more likely to comply than you would be if you saw a billboard or an ad in the paper.

Renewable Energy

• • • • •

If a school district wants to retain older buildings, they can still convert to renewable energy to operate their schools. Some schools are converting to wind power and some to solar. Flat school roofs lend themselves to photovoltaic installations, particularly in California, where there are large solar rebates in place. The Energy Commission of the state of California issued $4.5 million in its Solar School Program to thirty schools in the state of California. This helped to defray the cost of installing photovoltaic panels on the school roofs. The thirty subscriber schools combined will produce a total of 700 kilowatts of electricity, which will bring the state closer to its goal of producing 20 percent of its power from renewable sources.

The 2010 Imperative

• • • • •

At our local high school, I attended the 2010 Imperative, a satellite broadcast lecture on global warming, in January 2007. The New York Academy of Sciences and Ed Mazria, an architect who has been working on energy efficiency for the last thirty years, sponsored the 2010 Imperative. In the course of the broadcast, participants were invited to submit questions by computer. The broadcast was geared for sophisticated audiences and simulcast to forty-seven countries. However, the local seventh-grade science teacher felt it also would be important for his middle school class to attend. An eleven-year-old student submitted this question: "How can I make a difference in global warming?" The panel in New York responded that the student should go home and pose the same question to her parents. "Go home and ask them to turn down the thermostat and put on a sweater," one speaker suggested.

As a result of attending the 2010 Imperative, this class of seventh graders formed the "Global Heroes" club at their middle school and put a Power Point presentation together with the help of their science teacher. Their first presentation was to the school board, asking them to please do something about global warming. Later in the year they presented to the mayor, who had recently signed the Climate Protection Agreement, committing our town and county to reducing its energy footprint. They have been invited to so many different social clubs and gatherings that they have had to turn down invitations just to keep up their school attendance and complete their school work. There is no doubt that they will continue this work throughout high school and college. Once students are empowered to make a difference, they inspire others and the work continues. It is only when we get caught in despair that we become immobilized.

Green Hospitals

We think of our hospitals as healing places. The hospital is a place we go to get well after an emergency, surgery or serious illness. When our body has been compromised and our immune system is working overtime to fight to heal itself, we need daylight, fresh air and healthy surroundings. Unfortunately, hospitals often cause infections rather than curing them.

An estimated 88,000 deaths a year are attributed to hospital-caused infections.[6] Some possible contributors to infection may be lack of fresh air and toxic building and cleaning materials. Some of the tenets of green building that work to accelerate the healing process are daylight, fresh air and nontoxic building materials. It simply makes sense for our hospitals to support their patients in getting well as soon as possible.

Fortunately, there is a very active green hospital movement beginning in the United States. It involves totally new buildings, renovations of old buildings and an extensive new look at cleaning and waste management practices, including recycling.

Hospital Renovation
• • • • •

Hospital renovations include replacing vinyl floors with rubber floors, which require less maintenance, and replacing old HVAC systems with more modern systems that provide fresh-air exchanges rather than recirculation of old air. Hospitals are changing their lighting from outdated fluorescents to T-8 tubes, which last longer, use less electricity and deliver a better quality of light. They are using daylight wherever possible. When it comes time to paint, hospitals are moving away from the familiar institutional "hospital green" color and are using low VOC paints, stains and finishes. And they are switching to green cleaning products.

Green Cleaning
• • • • •

Hospitals want to reduce the incidence of infection, of course, so in the past they have used strong, sometimes toxic cleaning products, to disinfect all hospital surfaces. Some cleaning products contain possible carcinogens, others contain ingredients that cause asthma and bronchial and eye irritation. Hospitals that are going green realize that they must change their cleaning regimen so they do not cause further irritation to patients, hospital workers or the environment.

The Centers for Disease Control and Prevention has determined that it is not necessary to use disinfectants over all surfaces of a hospital and widespread use doesn't prevent infection. Disinfectants still must be used in specific areas where spread of infection is likely from blood and bodily fluids.

In June 2006, I was waiting in a hospital for my friend to come to his room after surgery and noticed a powerful, perfumed aroma wafting down the halls of the hospital. My nose began to run and my eyes burned. I asked the nurses about it. They said that the maintenance department had just sprayed a disinfectant into the air conditioning system and it was circulating throughout the hospital. I suggested that this might not be healthy for patients just waking up from surgery. Realizing the nurse was powerless to control this, we put a stack of towels on the air conditioner and kept the door to the hallway closed. The windows had been operable at one time, but were now bolted shut!

When patients are not subjected to toxic cleaning products, their bodies will recover faster, resulting in decreased length of hospital stays and expenses.

If your hospital is thinking of changing its cleaning protocol, there is a resource on the Hospitals for a Healthy Environment Web site that has a list of Ten Steps to Implementing a Green Cleaning Program.[7] Many hospitals have found that switching to green cleaning products has also saved them considerable amounts of money. It has also saved them from employee absenteeism because the workers who were using the toxic cleaning products are no longer suffering from chronic lung, skin and eye irritation caused by the old products. When patients are not subjected to toxic cleaning products, their bodies will recover faster, resulting in decreased length of hospital stays and expenses.

Recycling
• • • • •

Some hospitals are beginning to look at their entire waste stream and how it can be made more efficient. Many medical products are wrapped in packaging for single use only, which creates a great deal of waste. In Santa Cruz, California, nurses have been at the forefront of recycling. "Every time a baby was delivered in the maternal and child health unit at Dominican Hospital . . . nurses used three packages of supplies. Then Connie Gabriel-Wilson, RN, and other nurses in the unit convinced the supplier to consolidate those three packages into one, significantly reducing the volume of trash generated."[8] Packaging is a large part of municipal waste and "health care facilities generate 6,600 tons of waste a day"[9] largely due to increases in single-use packaging. It can be a bit more costly to buy sustainable products, but hospitals can combine with each other on their purchasing to reduce the amount of packaged products and also work with manufacturers to see if they can reduce waste and save money. Hospitals can actually make money on their recycling by selling some of the materials while saving money by reducing the volume of trash that would normally go to the landfill.

PVC
• • • • •

In the past, hospitals commonly burned their waste in an incinerator, but it was discovered that much of the waste emits toxic gases when burned. When polyvinyl chloride (PVC) is burned, it creates dioxin, which is one of the most toxic chemicals known to man. PVC is used in IV tubing and also in blood bags. In addition, PVC tubing is softened by diethylhexyl phthalate (DEHP), which can leach into IV tubing or blood bags, proving particularly harmful to neonatal infants.

Green hospitals are looking into alternatives to PVC and DEHP, and also are no longer incinerating their waste.

Mercury
• • • • •

Mercury has been used for a long time in thermometers and blood pressure cuffs because of its remarkable properties to tolerate high temperatures and pressures. Mercury is the only metal that is in a liquid state at normal temperatures. The downside of mercury is that it cannot be disposed of in an environmentally friendly way. Many hospitals are starting programs to replace mercury with mercury-free devices and instruments. There is an excellent step-by-step program for eliminating mercury at www.h2e-online.org, which will help you and the hospital staff methodically eliminate mercury from your hospital and replace it with safer, less toxic devices and chemicals.

The problem with mercury, and the reason its use should be discontinued, is that it is a bioaccumulative toxin. Once mercury gets into a stream, it is converted by bacteria into the organic form of methylmercury. Small organisms can ingest methylmercury in oceans, rivers and streams. Those organisms in turn are food for fish; the mercury accumulates at higher and higher levels as it ascends the food chain—"millions of times higher than the water they are swimming in."[10] In 2003, there were fish contamination advisories in forty-four of the fifty United States. Some states simply do not have the money to monitor their fish, which does not necessarily mean they are safe.

When a woman of childbearing age has high levels of mercury in her blood, the mercury can easily pass through the placental barrier and impact the fetus as a neurotoxin.

New Green Hospitals
• • • • •

New green hospitals are being built all over the country. Citizens, hospital boards and administrators are making the effort to create a healing environment that will save money and promote the highest health for patients and workers. Two of the first green hospitals in the country were Boulder, Colorado, Community Hospital's Foothill campus, which was the first hospital to receive the LEED Silver certification, and Newberg Hospital in Oregon that qualified for LEED Gold.

Action Points
• • • • •

In order to receive LEED certification, a hospital must take several things into account in its design process:

➲ The siting of the hospital should be a setting that restores an urban wasteland to useful land or preserves open space in the country.

➲ The building should be sited to maximize its solar potential both for passive and active solar heating.

➲ Construction materials must be safe, durable and nontoxic for the construction workers and the residents of the new hospital.

➲ Inside the hospital, floors, walls and cabinets must be built using nontoxic but durable green materials. Rubber floors instead of

PVC floors require less maintenance and do not require the constant waxing and stripping that PVC floors require.

- ⮑ Low or no VOC paints, stains, adhesives and carpets must be used.
- ⮑ Energy efficiency is a key component because unlike office buildings and schools, hospitals must run at peak efficiency twenty-four hours a day. Hospitals use large amounts of energy for heating, cooling and lighting, so it is important that these features are designed to operate and be maintained at maximum energy efficiency.
- ⮑ Additional exterior green features on the outside of a hospital include "green roofs," which minimize storm-water runoff, rain catchment systems that capture water for plant irrigation, and xeriscaping, which uses drought-resistant plants to landscape parking lots and exterior spaces.
- ⮑ Parking lots are paved with pervious pavers, which capture water rather than send it to storm drains.
- ⮑ Green hospitals also offer bike storage and shower rooms to encourage a green commute for their employees.

Studies have shown that "patients heal faster with natural light and windows that look outside."[11] Hospitals have also found that including plants, fountains and lots of sunlight helps patients feel healthier sooner.

Similar benefits are surfacing for employee retention that I mentioned earlier in the schools section of this chapter. Green hospitals have a decreased employee absentee rate, which can translate into thousands of dollars saved a year. Also, employees like working in a green building, so they keep their jobs longer, which saves thousands of dollars in job re-training costs.

Other savings that are proven in green buildings are the energy savings. This is particularly important for hospitals because they sometimes need to run on an emergency generator if the grid goes down. If a hospital is designed to run with maximum efficiency, then the generator will not be so taxed, and it will be able to generate for longer periods of time, until the grid is back in operation. Energy savings of up to 30 percent a year can easily offset the increased cost of building green.

The combination of less costly and nontoxic cleaning products, increased revenues from recycling, increased employee retention and accelerated patient healing all add up to a very attractive bottom line for green hospitals.

In addition, there are tax incentives, solar rebates, utility subsidies and grant programs that make it possible to obtain and pay off financing in a timely manner.

CHAPTER 5

Cars, Trains and Planes: Energy Solutions

"There are no passengers on spaceship Earth, only crew."

—Marshall McLuhan

Since the dawn of civilization we have been looking for better ways to transport ourselves and conduct commerce from place to place. The invention of the wheel, the Native American travois, the first steam engine, the model T Ford and the airplane—all increased our mobility and broadened our horizons. Before we had knowledge of global warming, or the impacts of fossil fuel on our atmosphere, we kept expanding into bigger and "better" vehicles and modes of transportation.

Now we realize that our unlimited mobility has a price. Transportation is responsible for about 30 percent of America's carbon footprint. In other words, 30 percent of all carbon dioxide emitted in the United States comes from the transportation sector. The emissions of the transportation sector fall just behind those of the building sector and are quite significant, given our population size. The nonprofit organization Environmental Defense reports that "The United

States has 5% of the world's population and 30% of the world's automobiles, but the country contributes 45% of the world's automotive CO_2 emissions."[1]

What to Consider about Your Car
• • • • •

If we just examine personal automobile usage, there are three main factors that should be considered:

1. The amount of driving that we do; i.e., transportation miles driven.

2. The fuel economy of the vehicles driven.

3. The carbon content of the fuel used to operate the vehicle.

These three main factors, combined together, can make a large difference in our carbon footprint. Consider number one. As individuals we have the most control over the amount of driving we do. We can choose to drive less. We can bike, walk or take the bus or train to work. If we live too far from work or public transportation, we can carpool to work or arrange to work at home some of the time. We can choose to combine trips with neighbors and plan our errands to minimize trips.

Number two, fuel economy, is also something within our control when we purchase a vehicle. The Toyota Prius hybrid gets about 55 miles to the gallon. The total carbon emissions from a Prius, if driven about 10,000 miles in a year, are 3,522 pounds of carbon dioxide. The average car manufactured by General Motors gets 19.2 miles to the gallon and produces about 12,000 pounds of carbon dioxide a year.[2] We must put pressure on our government, our legislators and on Detroit to change the Corporate Average Fuel Economy (CAFE) standards of the automobiles that are manufactured in the United States. Environmental Defense President Fred Krupp says, "Fixing the global warming problem without making cars more efficient is like trying to fix a leaky roof with a hammer. . . . The leading automakers must accept responsibility for becoming part of the solution."[3]

Carbon emissions from a Prius, if driven about 10,000 miles in a year, are 3,522 pounds of carbon dioxide. The average General Motors car gets 19.2 miles to the gallon and produces about 12,000 pounds of carbon dioxide a year.

Auto manufacturers have been successful for many years in defeating any legislation to increase CAFE standards. The Alliance of Automobile Manufacturers, which is the trade association that represents GM, Ford, DaimlerChrysler, Toyota and BMW, spends millions of dollars running TV and radio ads that portray soccer moms and farmers saying that they will have to pay much more money for a car if fuel economy standards are increased. The ads intend to send fear into the hearts of Americans by saying that moms won't be able to choose a "safe" car anymore if fuel economy standards are increased. The ads run in the states that sell the largest number of SUVs. Despite all this effort, on June 20, 2007, the Senate passed an energy bill raising CAFE standards by 40 percent to thirty-five miles per gallon by 2020. The House and the president of the United States must concur before this becomes law.

The third point to consider about your automobile is the carbon content of the fuel. As new flex-fuel vehicles become available that run on a mixture of 85 percent ethanol and 15 percent gasoline, the amount of fossil fuel used will decrease. As additional options such as biodiesel, hydrogen fuel cell and plug-in hybrid electric (PHEV) become available, we should be able to significantly reduce the carbon content of the fuel we use because we will be substituting either ethanol, biodiesel, hydrogen or electricity in the form of batteries for petroleum products, thus producing less carbon dioxide when combusted. David Freeman states in his book, *Winning our Energy Independence*, that "by far the most important action consumers can take involves the kind of motor vehicle an individual or company purchases. Consumers need to demand a plug-in hybrid or flex-fuel car and use biofuels for the internal combustion engine. If the dealer doesn't have it to sell, tell them you are not buying a new car or fleet till they or someone else offers one. The people, collectively, have the purchasing power, and withholding it until you get what you want can be a very effective tool for change."[4]

Other Countries Have Good Cars, Why Don't We?
• • • • •

The technology is already available for cars and light trucks to get better mileage. Cars and trucks in many other countries use fuel economy technologies without big price tags and without endangering the safety of their drivers. There are 113 different cars available outside the United States that get forty-plus miles to the gallon because the price of fuel is so much higher in many countries. Only two highly energy efficient automobiles are available for purchase in the United States: the Toyota Prius and the Honda Civic. Both are hybrids getting fifty or more miles per gallon. Hybrids have batteries that are charged by braking action and use a combination of gas and electricity generated from the battery for their power. Almost two-thirds of the fuel efficient models available overseas are manufactured by U.S.

automobile companies, GM and Ford, and foreign manufacturers have large U.S. markets, like Toyota, Volkswagen and Nissan. So a choice for Americans could be available.

The Legal Solution

In April 2007, a landmark decision by the U.S. Supreme Court stated that the EPA does have the jurisdiction to regulate greenhouse gas emissions from motor vehicles. However, since the court's decision, the EPA has still not moved to permit pending legislation to be enacted, which would allow states to regulate motor vehicle emissions. On May 30, 2007, Governor Schwarzenegger of California issued a statement at an EPA hearing that read, "Under the Clean Air Act, California has the right to enact its own air pollution standards. . . . Scientists have been telling us about climate change and global warming for years and we know the effect that greenhouse gases have. I see it already in California with the greater risk of forest fires, reduction in our snow-pack, higher smog levels, more flooding in the winter and hotter temperatures in the summer. The U.S. EPA must grant California a waiver without further delay."[5] We await developments.

There will have to be combined efforts of grassroots organizations, nonprofits like Environmental Defense, and the environmentally aware public, with governmental entities like the State of California, to begin to make a difference in the transportation sector's contribution to global warming. The American appetite for huge gas-guzzling cars and trucks is fueled by clever advertisers that lead us to believe we need large amounts of power and metal to propel ourselves safely down the highway. As long as Americans buy large SUVs and powerful trucks, Detroit will keep making them and send part of their corporate profits as campaign contributions to encourage Congress to keep the laws weak, CAFE standards minimal and the Clean Air Act ineffectual.

Plug-In Hybrid Electric Vehicles
• • • • •

One of the most promising technologies we will see soon is the plug-in hybrid electric vehicle (PHEV). Several of these PHEVs are being driven and demonstrated by a nonprofit group called Calcars, which has retrofitted the Toyota Prius to get 100 miles to the gallon.[6] Other PHEVs are being developed by GM with their Chevrolet Volt and by DaimlerChrysler with its Sprinter Van. All of these technologies are in test mode and not yet commercially available. The most exciting aspects of PHEVs are their reduced emissions of almost 60 percent less carbon dioxide, their fuel savings and their increased range to operate exclusively as an electric vehicle. PHEVs will likely be available in low-volume commercialization by 2012, and widely available by 2015.[7]

Most of the delay in introduction results from the development and testing of the lithium ion battery. At the present time hybrid vehicles (HVs) such as the Toyota Prius, are equipped with nickel metal hydride (NiMH) batteries, which assist the engine when it needs power and also operate electrically when the car is stopped or backing up. NiMH batteries are heavy, take up a lot of room and are not particularly suited to the deep cycle charging that will be necessary with a plug-in vehicle.

Enter the lithium ion battery, which is lighter, takes up less space, can be arranged in small battery packs and will be more suited to the recharging that will be necessary in a PHEV. PHEVs will operate on electricity for many more miles than their non-plug-in cousins. If the car's speed exceeds a certain level, the gas engine will kick in. The

100-miles-per-gallon estimate will depend on the driver's use patterns and ability to recharge the batteries. Right now it is estimated that a PHEV will have a range of 200 miles before it needs a charge. Many office buildings now being built are already including plug-in facilities in anticipation of a fleet of PHEVs parking and charging their batteries while employees are at work.

The most exciting aspects of PHEVs are their reduced emissions of almost 60 percent less carbon dioxide, their fuel savings and their increased range to operate exclusively as an electric vehicle.

Of course, it is important to take the entire energy picture into account. There is no point in saving energy and greenhouse gas emissions by driving a PHEV, only to plug it into the electrical grid that is fueled by a coal-fired plant belching greenhouse gases into the atmosphere. Solar energy is an obvious option.

California is starting to design covered parking with solar panels or film on the flat roofs that can recharge a car battery without using conventional energy. When a PHEV owner is recharging their batteries, it is recommended that the car be plugged in at night when grid demand is lowest. If a home has solar panels, or wind power, so much the better. Renewable energy can be the source of the electricity that recharges the batteries and not the conventional electrical grid.

Before the PHEV technology comes on line, you will be able to put a solar film roof panel on your Prius, which will extend the electrical mileage of a Prius to a range of twenty miles, and increase gas mileage by about 30 percent. There will be no plugs, just an extra battery in the rear.[8]

Presently, it is estimated that if the cost of gasoline is at $4 in 2012, the payback period on a PHEV would be four years. The lithium ion battery could increase the cost of an HV by $3,100. That is not a huge increase for a Toyota Prius that costs $24,000 in 2007, and represents an investment with a future return. By comparison, the Honda Hydrogen car costs $180,000 and other hydrogen cars are priced over $1,000,000, which indicates that hydrogen technology's cost effectiveness is a bit farther away than plugging in your hybrid.

Hydrogen
• • • • •

Hydrogen may well be the fuel of the future, not just for our cars, but as a source to generate electricity for our homes, for fuel cells and to propel airplanes. Automobile manufacturers are working with hydrogen fuel cell autos. One, the Honda FCX, has been leased to various cities and environmental agencies that are testing its performance. In 2008, the FCX concept car will be available for lease in a wider market.

The advantage of using hydrogen as a fuel is that it really is a zero-emissions fuel. Water vapor is all that comes out of the tailpipe of a hydrogen vehicle. Hydrogen fuel cell vehicles appear to be in our distant future, perhaps not commercially available until 2020 or 2025.

One of the problems is that hydrogen is presently produced with nonrenewable energy. President Bush has suggested that we use fossil fuels and even nuclear energy to manufacture hydrogen and turn it into usable electricity. This would be equivalent to "solving a problem at the level at which it was created," something that Einstein proved could not be done.

There are various experiments in hydrogen production going on around the country. Some are using electrolysis that introduces electricity into water to split out the hydrogen ions from the oxygen atoms. This would appear to be a great method, but it uses immense amounts of electricity to split the hydrogen. Alternative methods use concentrated solar energy to split out the hydrogen, and still others use wind. None of these methods is commercially viable at the moment, but there is hope for the future. Issues of flammability, storage under pressure and cost also remain to be solved.

Research to produce hydrogen using renewable fuel methods is of interest also, but it may be lacking in funding as most of the funding is going into producing hydrogen from natural gas. Once again, we are using fossil fuels, which will be exhausted in the future, to produce hydrogen, a nonpolluting alternative.

In the meantime, research will continue around the world. Iceland has a viable hydrogen-fueled public transportation system. The buses in Reykjavik run on hydrogen, and refueling stations are currently operating. Iceland generates the bulk of its energy from geothermal, and hopes to be totally dependent on hydrogen for transportation in the future. "By 2050, 100 percent of all motor vehicles must run on hydrogen, according to their plan."[9]

Flex Fuel
• • • • •

The manufacture of ethanol has received a lot of press lately, and also has received large government subsidies. The Bush administration and Congress feel that producing ethanol is both a way to keep the agricultural industry thriving and a way to solve our energy problems. In 2007, the Department of Energy provided $385 million to fund the construction of six new ethanol plants. However, some are questioning whether ethanol really is the magic bullet that will solve our energy problems.

A recent study at Stanford University reports that the by-products of ethanol will cause harmful pollution and endanger our air quality.

Ethanol is a form of alcohol that is derived from distilling fibrous plants. Most ethanol in the United States is produced from corn. Corn takes a lot of land to grow, robs nutrition from the soil and requires large amounts of fossil fuel to cultivate and harvest. Some say corn ethanol takes more energy to produce than it can generate. Fossil fuel–burning tractors are used to plant, fertilize and harvest corn. In addition, petroleum is the basis for the synthetic fertilizers, herbicides and pesticides used to grow corn. Once corn is harvested, it is sent by truck or train to refineries. These refineries use either natural gas or coal to distill the corn into alcohol-based ethanol. You get the picture?

There are also those who worry that so much corn is being used to generate ethanol that it is driving up the cost of food and is reducing corn as a source of food for humans and animals. Sugar beets are also used for the production of ethanol with similar effects. The government has suggested that we use more suitable ethanol sources such as switchgrass and other cellulosic waste products. These are not food products but are currently not commercially available in large quantities. Brazil, which is the world's number-one ethanol producer, uses sugar cane for its ethanol and runs a large number of its vehicles on this alcohol fuel.

Beyond the controversy surrounding the production of ethanol and its efficiency, there are questions of its efficacy as a non-pollutant. A recent study at Stanford University reports that the by-products of ethanol will cause harmful pollution and endanger our air quality. "Ethanol is being promoted as a clean and renewable fuel that will reduce global warming and air pollution," said Mark Z. Jacobson, the study's author and an atmospheric scientist at Stanford. "But our results show that a high blend of ethanol poses an equal or greater risk to public health than gasoline, which already causes significant health damage."[10] At a time when asthma rates are skyrocketing and air quality laws are being gutted, perhaps we should look with a wary eye at the expansion of ethanol as a fuel for the future.

Biodiesel

● ● ● ● ●

Biodiesel is a clean renewable fuel usually made from soybean oil that does not contain any petroleum products in its pure form. Biodiesel is made by a process called transesterification that separates glycerine from vegetable oil fat. Methyl ester is the technical name for biodiesel, and the glycerine by-product can be made into soap. Biodiesel is a commercially available fuel that has been approved for sale by the EPA.

One of the great things about biodiesel is that it produces significantly less greenhouse gases when it is combusted than traditional diesel. In its pure form, B-100, it produces 67 percent less carbon dioxide, virtually no sulfur dioxide, which is the gas that causes acid rain, and a bit more nitrogen oxide than traditional diesel. Biodiesel can be used to run buses, automobiles, tractors and any machine that would normally take diesel for a fuel.

In cold climates, biodiesel must be mixed with petroleum diesel to keep the fuel from forming into a gel. Most users of biodiesel run a blend called B-20, which is 20 percent biodiesel and 80 percent petroleum-derived diesel. Imagine what happens to a bottle of olive oil when you put it into the refrigerator. At temperatures below freezing, biodiesel starts to gel. Several ski areas, in an attempt to be green, use biodiesel to run their ski trail grooming equipment, but they have found that it is only feasible to run the mixture B-5, which is only 5 percent biodiesel. All ski area grooming is done at night when the temperatures are the coldest. You have to hand it to them for trying to make a difference!

One of the great things about biodiesel is that it produces significantly less greenhouse gases when it is combusted than traditional diesel.

"Veggie Mobiles" operate on french fry grease, collected from restaurants, but veggie oil is not a legal fuel. It is being manufactured around the country in homegrown biodiesel labs and fueling a small fleet of renewable energy vehicles. Do not try to pour grease from McDonald's directly into your gas tank! Running a vehicle on veggie oil is possible, but it requires a conversion kit for your diesel car or truck. These kits cost about $1,000 and there are Web sites that will help you through the installation process. It is imperative that you have the capacity to switch from veggie oil back to diesel so that your engine does not clog up when you turn off your vehicle. Veggie oil drivers love the smell of french fries coming out of their tailpipes!

Trucking

• • • • •

Much of the commerce in the United States requires trucks. Large semitrucks run on diesel fuel, and truckers are required by law to rest every day. In order to have a good rest, the truck engine must idle while the trucker is asleep. For the trucker's comfort, it is necessary to run a heater or air conditioner, or other appliances like a microwave or refrigerator. Idling gets a trucker zero miles to the gallon and also produces pollution. "About 500,000 heavy duty long-haul diesel trucks with sleeper cabs travel the United States. . . . It is estimated that the idling of long-haul trucks burns nearly a billion gallons of diesel a year, releasing significant amounts of air pollution and increasing fuel and maintenance costs to the truck owner."[11]

In 2007, there were eleven states that offered electrical plug-in outlets at truck stops so truck drivers would not have to idle their engines. Clean Cities, a nonprofit branch of the Department of Energy, is working to establish more of these facilities across the county. There are Web sites that can help a trucker find locations.[12]

For $10, truckers can buy a window retrofit that will allow them to use services that provide fresh air, heat, cooling and a variety of options so they do not have to idle their truck engines.

Airplanes

• • • • •

Airplanes produce a great deal of carbon dioxide at high altitudes. Sir Richard Branson, who owns half of Virgin Atlantic Airlines, has pledged $3 billion of his Virgin Group profits to help reach a solution to global warming. As part of his pledge, Virgin Atlantic Airlines is experimenting with towing airplanes to the takeoff runway instead of starting the engines at the gate. "Virgin said a reduction in 120,000 tonnes in carbon emissions a year could be made if extended across the fleet."[13] The experiment will begin at Heathrow and Gatwick airports in the United Kingdom and will extend to other airports.

Since the Hindenburg dirigible exploded in a fiery disaster in 1937, there was a belief that hydrogen was too dangerous for air travel. It is now understood that the skin of the dirigible caught on fire first, and then the hydrogen exploded, not the other way around. As hydrogen becomes a viable fuel for automobiles, it may also become commercially viable to fuel airplanes, which will significantly cut the emission of greenhouse gases into the atmosphere.

Boeing is experimenting with a fuel cell airplane that uses hydrogen and lithium ion batteries. It will be tested in Spain in 2007. At this time, Boeing does not envision the hydrogen fuel cell becoming the technology for commercial airliners. Geoffrey B. Holland and James J. Provenzano have a different perspective in their book, *The Hydrogen Age: Empowering a Clean-Energy Future*. Holland and Provenzano say that jetliners using hydrogen will "deliver improved performance, require less maintenance, and have a longer operational life mostly because with hydrogen fuel, there are no combustion residues left in the engine."[14] Airbus is also working on new designs for hydrogen aircraft. Unlike hydrogen cars that already have a projected market year, the forecasts are unclear for hydrogen jetliners.

Light Rail

Salt Lake City has a smog problem. Bordered by mountains that contribute to temperature inversions in winter, the mountains sometimes disappear from view. To reduce smog and congestion on the highways, the Utah Transit Authority (UTA) proposed to build a light rail line along the Wasatch Front, from Salt Lake City to Sandy, Utah. The idea was put to a vote and the referendum failed. But the UTA prevailed; it obtained some federal funding and local tax revenue, and the line opened in 1999, although clouded by controversy over whether it would be a success. Projected ridership was 14,000 passengers a day; the system has exceeded that since day one. The ridership has leveled out at about 21,000 passengers a day, which is 50 percent more than the best projections. In 1995, Salt Lake's Olympic bid was accepted and a new line was proposed from downtown to the University of Utah. It also was met with skepticism and controversy, particularly because it required rebuilding a main city street to construct the line. The new mayor, Rocky Anderson, smoothed the troubled waters, and the line opened two months before the Olympics. The UTA borrowed extra light rail cars from Dallas, Texas, for handling the crowds at the Olympics, and it was a great success.

Now that residents have seen the success of both the city and the commuter line, surrounding counties have approved additional tax revenues to take the commuter rail north to Ogden and south to Provo. These lines, including one to the airport, should be completed in 2008.

Mayor Rocky Anderson learned from the controversy that took place over the construction of the downtown line and has now

(Continued . . .)

added a construction mitigation clause to all of the new rail contracts. As the rail construction passes through a particular district, a community coordination team gets to vote on whether the construction crew has done their job well by keeping traffic moving and access to businesses available. If so, the contractor gets a bonus. This construction mitigation scheme has been such a hit, other cites are hiring the Salt Lake City consultant to help them design a similar program.

Action Points for Starting Light Rail

● ● ● ● ●

⮑ Start the planning process early.

⮑ Be sure all of the players are on board: the mayor, city council, residents and businesses that will be affected by the rail line.

⮑ Find out what opposition there is and bring all the players to the table to communicate.

⮑ Get financing in place. It usually is a combination of federal, state and local funds.

⮑ Sell the idea of taking cars off the road.

⮑ Publicize that creating clean air is important for our children. Light rail improves air quality.

⮑ Light rail is one contribution to solving the global warming problem.

⮑ Communities located next to light rail flourish.

⮑ Commuters are not car bound.

⮑ Transit-friendly housing is the wave of the future.

CHAPTER 6

Local, Organic, Sustainable Food

"Typically, 80 percent of our food dollars for industrial foods goes for processing, transportation, storage, packaging, and advertising and only 20 percent for the food itself. With care, almost anyone can find and afford good, local food."[1]

—John Ikerd, *Intelligent Food Economics*

One way our lifestyle choices can reduce global warming is to buy and source our food locally. Whether we plant a small container garden on the back steps of our apartment, several pots of herbs on our kitchen windowsill or pots on a porch or deck, we can have the satisfaction of growing and eating some of our own food. If we have the space, we can garden either on our land or in a community garden, where we can lease a small plot.

Many Americans are raising their own food and enjoying the satisfaction of pesticide-free food that they have nourished from seed to table. Gardening and growing plants can be a wonderful antidote to our stressful high-speed lifestyles. Working with the earth reminds us of our connection to nature and all living things. If you cannot grow any of your own food, you can support an organic farmer in growing your food. Start a farmers market in your community, or join a Community Supported Agriculture (CSA) farm, where you pay a share to the farmer in exchange for a weekly box of vegetables during the growing season.

The first share boxes from a CSA usually contain spring greens, which help to clean out the sluggishness in our bodies left over from winter. Eating foods that actually grow during that season is better for our bodies. We weren't meant to eat fruit salads from South America during the Minnesota winter. Fruits are a sugary, expansive food meant to cool down the body in the heat of summer. Joining a CSA can be a great way to eat local, fresh, seasonal produce, and keep your money circulating in your community.

Part of transportation's large carbon footprint has to do with the transportation of food. The average American dinner travels roughly 1,500 miles before it ends up on the dinner table.

When the CSA finishes its last deliveries in the fall and the farmers market closes, you can find local or regional farmers to provide you with your winter meals. If you eat meat, stock up on chicken, lamb, pork or beef, all grown organically close to home. Put them in your freezer or share a freezer with a neighbor and see how close to home you can eat for one winter. Many families are trying this experiment, only buying food from a 100- or 150-mile radius of where they live.

Barbara Kingsolver wrote a lyrical and wonderful book with her husband and daughter about their family's experiment growing their own food and eating locally in Virginia. The book is called *Animal, Vegetable, Miracle . . . A Year of Food Life*. She describes the adventures of clearing land, dealing with pests, getting to know the other local farmers and the culinary inventiveness that brought a sense of joy to her family. The book is also filled with informative facts, Web sites and references to help communities find a way back to local food production. "If every U.S. citizen ate just one meal a week (any meal) composed of locally and organically raised meats and produce, we would reduce our country's oil consumption by over 1.1 million barrels of oil every week. That's not gallons, but barrels. Small changes in buying habits can make big differences. Becoming a less energy-dependent nation may just need to start with a good breakfast."[2] When I first read this quote, I thought that Kingsolver's husband was suggesting that we fast and diet, eating only one meal a week, but I realized that he meant only one "organic" meal a week. Surely that would be easier to do in the summer, if you do not have a year-round farmers market. It could be as simple as a breakfast of locally raised eggs, a melon from your neighbor's community garden and muffins you bake yourself with blackberries that you've picked.

The point is that the typical supermarket food uses a tremendous amount of fuel before it is even trucked to the store. The farm equipment, pesticides and fertilizers all either consume fuel or are petroleum based. Once the food item is shipped to be processed or milled and shipped again to be packaged and shipped again to the distribution center and shipped again to your local supermarket—a great deal of fossil fuel has been consumed.

Part of transportation's large carbon footprint has to do with the transportation of food. The average American dinner travels roughly 1,500 miles before it ends up on the dinner table. A study from the University of Iowa says, "Examples of external environmental costs are the increased amount of fossil fuel used to transport food long distances, and the increase in greenhouse gas emissions resulting from the burning of these fuels. Local and regional food systems, where farmers and processors sell and distribute their food to consumers within a given area, may use less fossil fuel for transportation because the distance from farm to consumer is shorter."[3]

Roughly 17 percent of the nation's transportation cost is devoted to shipping food across the country. Since California is the main food producer and New York has the largest population concentration, that is a lot of heads of lettuce, which contain 94.9 percent water, being shipped across the country so New Yorkers can enjoy their salads.[4]

The use of fossil fuels and long-distance transport had very little to do with our food supply at the beginning of the twentieth century, when most food was locally grown and transported by wagon to the local market. Food was not sprayed with pesticides or grown with synthetic fertilizers until after World War II, when the petrochemicals that make up these materials became readily available.

In the late 1960s, the Green Revolution was launched to end world hunger. Funded by the Rockefellers and the Ford Foundation, agricultural scientists developed new strains of wheat, and found ways to ship fertilizers, pesticides and modern farm equipment all over the world. The Green Revolution did improve food distribution to remote locations, but it also led to population explosion in some poorer countries. The downside of the Green Revolution was the introduction of the widespread use of pesticides, fertilizers and mono cropping into countries that formerly grew and ate a variety of local foods. These supposedly advanced technologies radically changed the soil, water, local customs and dietary habits of vast numbers of people worldwide. As a result of switching to monocultures and double cropping, many of the world's poorer farmers were pushed off their land into the cities.

Several years after the Green Revolution occurred overseas, massive changes began to happen in U.S. agriculture. Sustainable Table reports "between 2005 and 2006, the United States lost 8,900 farms (a little more than 1 farm per hour)"[5] Despite these staggering statistics, approximately 3,500 family farms still exist.

There is a very large and heartening and growing movement alive in the United States that is producing organic food, distributing it locally and restoring family farms to productivity. The advantages to this localized effort are many. There are minimal transportation costs. If the food needs to be transported, it is for a very short distance. Organic farming does not use synthetically based pesticides or fertilizers, both of which are petroleum-derived products and can be harmful to the bodies of those who apply them to the food and the soil. Organic soil has an abundant number of nutrients composed of vitamins and minerals that are transferred into our bodies through eating healthy food. The closer the food is grown to home, the better chance we have that the nutrients will still be in the food. You know the difference between the taste of a tomato picked from your tomato vine and popped into your mouth versus a Flavr Savr tomato that has been genetically modified with a fish flounder gene so that it can withstand cold temperatures and crush less easily. And then it is shipped 1,500 miles from an industrial farm in California only to sit on the produce aisle for a week or two before you eat it. There is no comparison.

Presently, we have no idea what the consequences of eating genetically modified foods might be. In the United States, foods do not have to be labeled if they contain genetically modified organisms (GMOs). In fact, "over 70 percent of all nonorganic foods in the United States already contain GMOs."[6] If we want to be sure we are not eating GMO food, it just makes sense to eat as organically and locally as we can.

We pay three times over for seemingly "cheaper" nonorganic products—once at the counter, again with our taxes for farm subsidies, and again to clean up the environmental degradation caused by the chemicals used on nonorganic farms that end up in our water table, streams and rivers.

Many family farms have shifted from mono cropping with pesticides to organic farming. To meet organic farming standards, the farm, its soil, its produce, livestock and processing practices must all meet U.S. Department of Agriculture (USDA) guidelines.

The farm must be free from all synthetic pesticides, fertilizers, antibiotics and growth hormones. The cost of nonorganic farming has risen because the cost of fossil fuels has risen, but often nonorganic farmers receive subsidies for their farms while organic farmers do not. Many consumers complain about the high cost of organic food. Some use the nickname of "whole paycheck" when they speak of Whole Foods markets. The truth is that we are also paying hidden costs for that Flavr Savr industrially grown tomato. We pay three times over for seemingly "cheaper" nonorganic products—once at the counter, again with our taxes for farm subsidies, and again to clean up the environmental degradation caused by the chemicals used on nonorganic farms that end up in our water table, streams and rivers.

Organic agriculture takes the whole picture into account. The health of the soil, the health of the animals, the practice of integrated pest management and the delivery of a healthy product to the consumer are all key. It makes sense that doing something in a careful sensitive way may cost more, initially just like green building discussed in chapter three. The benefits represent tremendous savings that occur later and may not be factored into the initial price. Some of the benefits of organic, local agriculture are the decreased carbon footprint of organic vegetables and meat, the increased health benefits to ourselves and our children, the satisfaction of eating food we have raised ourselves, and the healthy soil, air, rivers and streams that nourish the ecosystems of our food. None of these benefits are factored into the cost when we pay for an organic product, and yet they should be.

Starting a CSA
• • • • •

The community supported agriculture movement is growing by leaps and bounds. In 1990, in the United States there were fifty CSAs, while by 2005, there were at least 1,500. The setup of a CSA can vary from community to community and with each region of the country, but basically an individual, restaurant or family buys a "share" of the farm.

Ideally, the share would be bought in the fall or winter, which gives the farmer capital to finance and plan for the next summer's crop. Tractors can be upgraded, seeds bought, greenhouses built over the winter, all with the shareholder's money. Then from spring to fall, boxes of food will be delivered weekly or shares can be picked up at distribution points or from the farm directly.

The idea of the community supporting farmers originated in Japan in the 1960s when a group of women became concerned about the volume of food imports to their community and the demise of small farmers. They started what was called a "teikei," which means "putting the farmer's face on food." This was so successful that it was replicated in Europe and later in the United States.[7]

I joined my first CSA in 1988, after moving to northern California. The farm was far from my house. In fact, I never went there, but the deliveries were left on my front porch once a week. It was the high point of the week for my family to open the box and discover what was inside. A basket of raspberries would not last five minutes as we sat down on the floor and ate them all before unpacking the rest of the box. We learned about strange greens we had never seen before, like kohlrabi and bok choy. Each week, the farm would include a folksy newsletter that included recipes. The farm would tell us what to anticipate for the following week, so we were really looking forward to our first farm tomatoes. The next week's box arrived with no tomatoes and the newsletter's apology, saying that a black bear had wandered into the tomato patch and had quite a picnic! The vines were trampled, the fruit squashed and eaten, and the harvest ruined. I had been under the impression that black bears were essentially extinct from California except in Yosemite, and also had no idea they ate tomatoes.

In addition to providing our family with healthy produce, my kids learned how to shuck corn and deal with corn weevils—*yucky, mom!*—how to make zucchini bread from giant zucchini, and how to integrate strange new veggies into their spaghetti. Even though we never visited the farm, we felt a sense of connection to the farmer who was raising our food, and a sense of sadness upon having to return to the supermarket for the winter months.

Now in Wyoming, where the growing season is quite short, we are blessed with several CSAs and dedicated farmers who fight the frost, work their fingers to the bone and deliver fresh produce from spring to fall. We bring our own bags to a distribution point where the veggies are spread out on a table. A white board tells us how much of each item to weigh and pick up.

Case Study

Cosmic Apple Gardens was started in Victor, Idaho, eleven years ago. At the time, the farmer, Jed, was working at a restaurant that received very sad-looking basil from the big food distribution truck supplying the restaurant. He saw the opportunity to grow some homegrown basil, so he built a greenhouse and has never looked back. The basil was such a successful crop that he began supplying other local restaurants, started a few other small crops and began to sell them at a farm stand, both in Idaho and over the border in Wyoming. One of the Wyoming customers convinced Jed to start a CSA. He began by leasing land from a small farm nearby and customers convinced their friends to buy shares in the CSA. The land had always been pesticide free, so Jed was well on his way to becoming an organic

(Continued . . .)

farmer, without the effort of letting the soil repair itself from years of mismanagement. In the early days up until 2005, organic farms could get a third party to certify to their customers that the farm practices were healthy, and the soil and plants were not treated with any synthetic pesticides or fertilizers. Then in 2005, the USDA started inspecting organic farms and requiring certain practices of the farmers. Unfortunately, the USDA did not see the wisdom in Jed saving his potato seeds from year to year that kept the potato strains organic and adapted to the particular location where they were grown. Because Idaho grows potatoes, the USDA made Cosmic Apple Gardens abandon their own seed and spend $1,000 to purchase seed so they wouldn't endanger their neighbors who grow seed potatoes commercially. Ahh, the wisdom of the federal government that subsidizes agribusiness to the tune of millions of dollars a year but imposes a hardship on a small organic farmer just to protect more agribusiness!

The USDA spends $1.5 million for the National Organic Program, but in contrast, it spent $37 million to subsidize farmers who grew dry peas. Consumers spend $14 billion a year on organic produce.[8]

Despite the USDA, the farm continues to flourish. Jed outgrew the leased land, and one of the CSA members worked hard to fund-raise and convince a generous donor to purchase a bigger piece of land where the farm is now located. Jed was given a book about biodynamic farming, which has refined his farming practices beyond organic farming. Biodynamic farming essentially creates a closed loop system on the farm so that the waste products get turned into compost; pigs and cows roam freely through a pasture that is then rotated into plants, and the wandering chickens eat the bugs that would otherwise eat the plants.

The principles of biodynamic farming originated with Rudolf Steiner in Austria in the 1920s, who taught that every living thing has a purpose. In biodynamic farming, crops are intermingled. Flowers are planted among the vegetables, fruits mix with potatoes, and bees are kept to pollinate all of the flowering plants. It is believed that fewer pests can live in this integrated atmosphere where plants are mixed together and the soil is healthy.

A strong plant will not be susceptible to pests, while a weakened plant in poor soil invites an infestation. Instead of mining the soil for maximum yield, the soil is nourished and treated as a living organism just like a cow or plant. Each has its life cycle; each has its own needs.

Cosmic Apple Gardens now has 200 shareholders who receive their veggies for sixteen weeks, from mid-June into October. The farm keeps a very low overhead with thirty work-share employees who work five hours a week for six months in exchange for one share of the farm produce. Unlike most farmers, Jed was never in debt until the old delivery truck broke down. He had to purchase a new truck, which now runs on biodiesel. He will pay off the truck in the next few years. The next big purchase will be buying the land from the donor who bought it for them. They hope to find a grant program to help them with this purchase.

Some of the activities that build community within a CSA are:

1. The farm day when members can visit, share a potluck meal and listen to good music into the night.

2. Asking members to host a drop-off site, overseeing the distribution of produce, answering questions and welcoming the shareholders to yet another feast of healthy food.

(Continued . . .)

3. Publishing a newsletter that accompanies each delivery. Ours has wonderful hand drawings of fanciful veggies, recipes, news of the farm and its animals, and tips for handling and storing the food. Every week includes "The Dressing Room," with yet another exotic salad dressing recipe.

4. A member has created a nonprofit foundation to educate kids about organic farming. She has secured a grant to plant a children's garden and also to build a field bathroom.

5. Cosmic Apple's participation in the local farmers market, which is held in our town for ten weeks during the summer, builds awareness about the farm, enables selling excess produce to introduce non-member residents to the farm, and affords an opportunity to sign up new shares for the following year.

Case Study 2

Farmer John, who grew up on a farm in Caledonia, Illinois, runs one of the largest CSAs in the country with 1,200 members and twenty distribution sites in the Chicago area. People from Chicago who loved his produce came to him, asking him to start a CSA. At first he refused. If you worked a ninety-hour week, you might refuse a new idea too! It took some time and volunteer help for Farmer John to see the wisdom in the CSA movement. Once he committed to it, his farm took off. After years of struggle, the loss of the farm and the return to it, Farmer John and the farm are now flourishing. He offers classes for the next generation of farmers. He also offers programs that help fund shares for low-income residents of Chicago who want access to healthy food but do not have that access in the inner city. The farm educates children, teaches cooking classes and makes soap from goat's milk.

Action Points

• • • • •

⊃ Start small, raising a few successful plants at home. Herbs, a few lettuces and radishes are foolproof.

⊃ Think about where your food comes from. Are your apples from New Zealand, Chile or Oregon? Do you buy strawberries and bananas all winter long?

⊃ Take your own bag to the market, neither paper nor plastic are good options for bringing our food home. Your own canvas bag will save trees and help stop the plastic proliferation we see hanging from our trees and plastered against fences.

⊃ Find a neighbor to share trips to the store, put a basket or rack on your bike or take the bus. Plan ahead so you don't have to make several trips to the store.

⊃ Start a food co-op to order foods in bulk and share them with your community.

⊃ Start a farmers market; it can be small and fun, and it supports local food.

⊃ Start a CSA, support a local farmer and keep the food dollars in your community.

⊃ Pay attention to your fast-food diet. How do you feel when you rush by the takeout window and eat in your car? See the film *Fast Food Nation*.

⊃ Talk to your kids about their diet, where foods come from and how foods nourish the body. Get exercise and fresh air; you will want to eat better food after that.

⊃ Don't get discouraged. Changing our eating habits takes time. Start slowly and add what you can afford over the period of a year or two. Once you switch to healthy food, you will notice the difference and not want to turn back!

CHAPTER 7

Save Water, Recycle

"Thousands have lived without love, not one without water."

—W. H. Auden

Water is becoming a precious resource. Something we have always taken for granted in the United States is becoming scarce. In the Rocky Mountain states, drought conditions for many years have changed the availability of water for drinking, agriculture and industry. Water is getting more expensive for many cities, towns and municipalities. Several factors are converging at once to complicate the water picture.

Global Warming
• • • • •

Although one of the effects of global warming is increased melting of glaciers, causing rising sea levels, there is no way to capture the fresh water melting into the ocean. As fresh water mixes with saltwater, low-lying lands are already flooding. When an island that has very little fresh water is flooded with saltwater, it could mean the end for the

89

inhabitants. Not only are freshwater ponds being flooded and sali-nated, but taro crops and palm trees are dying as the saltwater rises into their root structures. Taro and palm are two of the main food sources of many tropical island populations.

The Nobel Prize–winning Intergovernmental Panel on Climate Change reports that "water availability in Southern Europe may be reduced by 80 percent or more, leading to water shortages and dete-rioration of water quality."[1] National Geographic's Tim Appenzeller says, "Most glaciers in the Alps could be gone by the end of the cen-tury. Glacier National Park's namesake ice by 2030. The small gla-ciers sprinkled through the Andes and Himalaya have a few more decades at best."[2]

The reason for alarm is not just the loss of the glaciers with grave consequences for the alpine habitat and surrounding environment, but the villages and cities downstream from the glaciers that have depended on the water for hundreds of years will have to find other sources of water for their communities. In the United States, the effects will be mixed with some areas experiencing extreme drought coupled with forest fires and others flooding in ways not experienced for many years. Even in the north, the integrity of our water is threatened. The National Science Foundation (NSF) reports that nitrate levels in Lake Superior are on their way to making the water undrinkable. The NSF says, "The trend is a concern because Lake Superior contains 10 per-cent of the Earth's supply of surface fresh water." Part of the nitrate increase seems to come from naturally occurring decaying plant mat-ter and sewage, but the majority seems to come from agricultural fer-tilizers and fossil fuel combustion. Robert Sterner, the author of the study, says ". . . it's not too early to give this situation more attention."[3]

The UN warns that two-thirds of the earth's population will lack adequate water supplies by 2025.

Nitrates aren't the only problem plaguing Lake Superior. The lake level is at its lowest point in the last eighty years. Losing your lakeshore is hard on recreational boaters, but power plants are running at half their capacity, and the shipping industry is running with decreased loads. If a ship has to leave part of its load behind due to low water, it gets expensive. Adolph Ojard, executive director of the Duluth, Minnesota, Seaway Port Authority, says, "Cargo ships have lightened loads about 5%. For ships averaging $6 a cargo ton and making 40 trips a year, that amounts to about $1 million in lost revenue per ship."[4]

Some Minnesotans are reluctant to attribute the changes in the lake to global warming; they say it's just a drought. They are waiting for rain.

Whether we live in a place that is flooding or we are already rationing water due to drought, it never hurts to save water. We literally cannot live without it. Our bodies are made up of almost 90 percent water. We need to drink water every day to help the body function in an optimum way. Even if you don't drink the prescribed eight glasses of water a day, each of us would die of dehydration in a few days time if we had no access to water.

The UN warns that two-thirds of the earth's population will lack adequate water supplies by 2025, and one in five people do not have access to clean drinking water today. You may think "Well, that isn't me. I live by a lake or river and can use all of the water I want," but that may not always be the case. We never know when the aquifer we depend on will be drawn down. Water disappears when agriculture drills too many wells for irrigation. The water table can change if a golf course builds ponds and uses their sprinklers frequently, or when a water-intensive industry moves in next door and starts to affect the aquifer. River patterns change, and lakes and streams become polluted or lose their pH balance, which affects our drinking water. Cities and town water systems are realizing that they don't have the money to replace aging pipes and filtration systems, and that their water infrastructure is crumbling, and all of a sudden they have to raise water rates. We can all do our part by starting to be aware of our water use at home.

Ways to Conserve Water at Home
• • • • •

1. Turn your faucet off while brushing teeth, shaving, washing or rinsing dishes. There's no need to run the faucet to get water hot; get an electric tea kettle and heat it.

2. Check for leaks in seldom-used faucets and around old toilets and water heaters; notice if your water bill has suddenly jumped, and find the source.

3. Put water-saver aerators on your faucets, water-saver heads on your shower, and if you replace an appliance, make sure it is an Energy Star appliance. If you replace a toilet, find the one that uses the least amount of water. Many new toilets are dual flush.

4. Baths take thirty-six gallons of water, more water than showers, and hand washing your dishes can use more water than running a full low-water dishwasher every few days.

5. If you are landscaping, xeriscape, which means planting native drought-resistant plants and grasses. If you have a lawn, water at night or in the very early morning hours on a timer. Do not water during rainstorms.

6. Resist buying bottled water; if your tap water does not taste good, get a filter. If you carry water with you to work, get a stainless steel water bottle that will not leach plastic into your water. Never put plastic bottles in your freezer, or pour hot liquids into a plastic bottle; the plastics can leach into your drinking water. Disposable plastic water bottles are made from petroleum. They fill up our landfills, and the water costs us ten times more than gasoline for the same amount of liquid.

7. Avoid using your disposal. Start a home compost program. If you do not have a garden, take the compost to the community garden.

8. If you mow your lawn, leave it at least three inches long. The roots will not dry out or need as much water. Mulch, don't bag, your grass. Collect rainwater in a barrel and cover with a screen to avoid breeding mosquitoes; use it for watering your plants and bushes.

9. Go to a carwash that recycles its water. If you wash your car at home, get a shutoff valve for your hose and wash your car on the grass so the water is used twice. Use biodegradable soap.

10. Clean your driveway and sidewalk with a broom, not a hose.

Saving Water at Work
• • • • •

1. Ask for a water cooler that has both hot and cold water or use the tap.

2. Encourage water conservation at your workplace or office; it will save the business money.

3. Ask employees for suggestions on how to conserve water at work.

4. If your business is water-intensive, how can you recycle your gray water and use it again?

5. Work with your local water utility to find solutions to your business's high-water usage.

6. If you are designing a new business building, plant a green roof.

7. Design pervious pavers in the parking lot to catch water runoff and keep it out of storm drains.

8. Design rainwater catchment barrels so the runoff from the roof can be used again for watering plants.

9. If your business uses large amounts of hot water, plan to install solar thermal panels on the roof to preheat the water.

10. Install a heat exchanger to capture the heat of wastewater pipes.

Reduce, Reuse and . . .

• • • • •

The three Rs go together, but, ultimately, recycling should be our last resort. Someday we may reuse everything and have no need to recycle. See what you can reduce by looking at the packaging of an item before you buy it. Go without a bag or bring your own or buy from bulk bins or old-fashioned stores where items are not wrapped in two layers of hard plastic. We, as consumers, will change how things are packaged; don't count on industry to initiate the change.

Reuse all that you can. Clothes can be handed down or modified to be reused. Cut off the legs of pants to make shorts, turn old jeans into skirts, cut the neck and sleeves off a tee shirt to make a summer shirt. Reuse plastic bags instead of sending them to the landfill. Whole industries are being made out of recycled goods; seek them out and support them. Purses made out of seatbelts, coffee tables from bike parts, fleece baby clothes from the remnants of fleece jackets—all are efforts of ingenuity that deserve our dollars and support.

Recycle

● ● ● ● ●

Modern recycling programs in the United States began around the time of Earth Day in 1970. Until the Industrial Revolution, many items were reused at home and in businesses. Rags were turned into paper, metal was collected and made into tools, and food waste was compressed and made into soap. The first recycling bins appeared in New York City around 1897, but were removed in 1919. After the world wars, we became a disposable society, burning our garbage without attention to air quality, and creating dumps and landfills to bury our waste.

Much of New York City's waste was dumped directly into waterways surrounding New York until an ordinance forbade the dumping in 1934. After that, refuse was put on barges and towed out into the ocean for dumping. In the spring of 1987, a barge named *Mobro 4000* left Islip, New York, where the landfill was full, bound for North Carolina. When it got there, the barge was refused. The *Mobro* began a ludicrous six-month journey of trial and error to dump its contents, which were refused by "six states and three countries."[5] Ultimately, the refuse was brought back to New York and incinerated!

The Fresh Kills landfill was created on Staten Island in 1947 to receive New York's refuse. It is so large that it is visible from space with the naked eye. Fresh Kills was closed in 2001 and then reopened to receive the remains of the World Trade Center. There are now plans for Fresh Kills to become a park with trails, waterways, green spaces, a wind farm and a memorial to all who died at the World Trade Center.

Americans create a great deal of trash. Each day, each person throws away an average of 4.8 pounds of trash. Some of our trash is recyclable and compostable. We need programs in our communities to coordinate the collection and sale of our used goods.

Some cities were spurred into recycling by the closure of landfills and also the recognition that recyclable refuse could be lucrative. By 2003, recycling programs in the United States had diverted seventy-two million tons of goods from landfills. These numbers doubled from 1990, proving that recycling is a great idea and that it makes money. It just doesn't make sense to bury valuable materials in a landfill or burn them when they can be made into something else, and save energy and reduce pollution at the same time.

Each municipality is different and so there can be no generalization about recycling on a national scale. Each community must look at its waste stream and decide how and where they can sell the items collected. So much depends on the supply chain coming into the community and the markets for the goods they have collected. Markets for all recycled materials, such as glass or cardboard, fluctuate just like any commodity market.

Recycling's Effect on Global Warming

When aluminum is mined from bauxite to make cans, it is a very energy-intensive process that contributes to global warming. So every aluminum can recycled reduces the amount of CO_2 released into the atmosphere, and it saves the mineral resource from being mined as well. It takes a great deal less energy to turn that aluminum can back into another aluminum can, which is back on the shelf in ninety days. If a single aluminum can is recycled, it saves enough energy to power a 100-watt lightbulb for 3.5 hours, or 210 minutes, or the equivalent amount of energy equal to one cup of gasoline.

Trees are our friends; they sequester carbon. Each time we cut down trees, we are losing our ability to store the carbon that we release into the atmosphere. To make a ton of paper, it takes seventeen trees. Worldwide, we use 300 million tons of paper a year. Thirty-five percent of our trees are used in paper. In the United States, with only 5 percent of the world's population, we use 30 percent of the world's paper; that works out to about 749 pounds of paper per person per year. By using recycled paper, and recycling our newspapers and office papers, we can begin to make a dent in global warming and keep paper out of the landfill. Recycling also makes it possible for those communities that are still burning their waste to reduce the volume of their waste and shut down their incinerators.

It just doesn't make sense to bury valuable materials in a landfill or burn them when they can be made into something else, and save energy and reduce pollution at the same time.

Landfills generate methane that is a by-product of decomposition of waste, particularly food waste. If we compost our food and garden waste, this waste stays out of the landfill. Methane is one of the culprits in greenhouse gases that contributes to global warming. If we keep material out of the landfill, less methane will be generated. Some landfills have initiated methane-capture programs, where methane from the landfill runs a generator that can supply power to surrounding businesses.

Starting a Recycling Program in Your Community

A woman who was passionate about recycling started the Jackson Community Recycling Center in 1990. She also wanted to make a difference in the way the community handled waste. She did her homework and researched how other recycling centers worked across the country. The first step in getting any recycling program going is to speak to the local officials. It always helps to bring along other interested citizens to show that there is interest in the community to launch a new program. The sanitation department should be very familiar with the "waste stream" of the community; i.e., how much garbage is going to the landfill. They will know the tonnage of waste and the amount of recyclables that could be kept out of the waste stream if a program is started. The proposal to recycle should be music to the ears of any sanitation department, as getting rid of waste is expensive. Waste is either hauled by truck to a landfill nearby, or more often is shipped away to a distant site that costs the town or county money per ton of waste.

The way the program started in Jackson was with one drop-off site with several large reusable boxes; one for each item: aluminum cans, steel cans, glass bottles, newspaper, magazines and office paper. It is extremely important that you know you have a market for these items before you begin your program. It can make or break a recycling program to start collecting an item that you then cannot sell or have to send to the landfill. It is hard enough to convince people to recycle; you do not want to confuse them by getting them used to recycling cereal boxes, for example, and then telling them they cannot recycle them. So be certain there is a market for all the recyclables you collect before you launch your advertising campaign, and start putting out your collection bins.

Finding a Buyer and Shipping

The program in Jackson began by transporting its recyclables to a nearby town that already had buyers for recycled goods in place. Beginning your program like this is a good way to find out which mills buy what recyclables and how much they pay. You get a feel for the market and what sells over the period of a few years. Being in the recycling business is a bit like being a commodities broker. The price paid per ton for recycled goods is in a state of constant flux. You have to be able to absorb these price differences. For example, when the program began in 1990, a ton of newspaper was selling for $235 per ton. A year and a half later, it was selling for $5 per ton. Luckily, the recycling center had a good relationship with their buyer and the buyer kept picking up the bailed newspapers during the pricing slump.

Funding

It is important to get a buy-in from the town, city or county for funding your program. You are not asking for a handout because ultimately your center will be making money and saving the town or county money in tipping fees charged at the landfill. Over the last six years, Jackson Community Recycling has saved Teton County $1.2 million in fees it would have paid to send recyclable items to the landfill. The recycling center has made $1.6 million in revenues by selling goods to mills that recycle materials.

You will need some start-up money for salaries and collection boxes, and you want the elected officials to support the idea of your recycling program with their PR, policies, votes and dollars.

(Continued . . .)

The recycling center in Jackson is a public nonprofit. Teton County, the Town of Jackson and the nonprofit board of the center jointly govern it. If you are a nonprofit, or a government entity, you can receive donations from the community, and donors can deduct their contribution on their taxes.

Building

The start-up program was so successful that the director started looking for a permanent site where a processing facility could be built. The goal was to cut out the middleman and ship directly to end markets and to accommodate the enthusiasm for recycling. The planning began in 1991 and construction began in 1993. It is important that your facility be designed to accommodate increasing tonnages of recyclables from a growing population and also a growing interest in recycling.

The design of a sorting, or material recovery, facility is different from a drop-off facility. Be clear from the start about your needs and volume of materials and visit other processing facilities to assess your needs.

If you have a very large city, you may choose to commingle the recyclables. In other words, the city will hand out one bin to each resident and all recycling will go in this one bin; i.e., aluminum cans, newspapers, magazines, etc. The resident's bins will be picked up and sorted at a material recovery facility. You must have state-of-the-art sorting equipment and an endless guaranteed labor source—longevity of employees at these facilities is sometimes no more than a week. Be prepared to deal with almost as much garbage as recyclables, as people tend to dump everything imaginable into their recycling bins, in hopes that maybe what they've put in the bin is indeed recyclable.

If you begin with separated materials dropped off in bins and baled at the recycling center, that center requires a different kind of design. Jackson is a relatively small town with county residents numbering about 20,000 people. It did not make sense to build a sorting facility in 1993. It may make sense to expand some time in the future.

The recycling center is a 14,000-square-foot building that cost $1.2 million to build. It has a scale in the floor and room for conveyor belts, a baler and plenty of room for storage while the bales are awaiting shipping. There is also room for forklifts and trucks to maneuver inside the building.

Collection

Collection takes place at several drop-off sites around the county. These Community Recycling Sites are usually hosted on property owned by a business or individual, or the town or county. The bins are on trailers so they can be pulled to the recycling center on a weekly schedule. Ten years into the program, new and bigger roll-off containers have been ordered because the program has been so successful and the community has outgrown the bins on trailers.

The sites have clear signage explaining what recyclables go in each bin, with a separate bin for corrugated cardboard by the side. Again, be sure you have a market for something before you put out a bin for it. Many plastics can be difficult to market. The program in Jackson did not start by taking them but added them later, when they were sure they could sell them. There are still certain types of plastics that are not economical to sell such as any food or beverage container other than #1 and #2 bottles.

(Continued . . .)

Until Jackson Community Recycling can accept these plastic items for recycling, they educate the community to simply avoid purchasing items that are packaged in hard-to-recycle containers.

Trash Transfer Station

The recycling center works very closely with the county transfer station. The transfer station is run and funded by trash tip fees collected at the scale (currently $50 per ton). Since there is no longer a landfill in Teton County, the trash transfer station is where trash gets dropped off to be shipped to a landfill in another county eighty miles away. All construction waste is now required to be sorted so that it can be recycled or reused rather than sent to the landfill. Yard waste and landscaping material is chipped and/or composted along with waste lumber. Teton County's green and clear glass is crushed and used in projects by the county road and levee department. Although Teton County does not yet have a food composting program, there are many communities that do, and it may be possible in your area.

Electronic and Hazardous Waste

• • • • •

Most recycling facilities have special programs for electronic waste such as computers, TVs, old cell phones and microwaves. Many electronic devices contain heavy metals or other toxic components. It is important that these materials do not go to the landfill.

A material is considered to be hazardous waste if it contains toxic substances that could leach into the groundwater of a landfill. Paints, batteries, pesticides, herbicides, stains and fumigants, and burned-out or broken CFLs should all be taken to the hazardous waste day at your recycling center. Some facilities will take hazardous waste at any time if you notify them ahead of time; others have special collection days throughout the year.

Action Points

• • • • •

⊃ Talk to your local officials to get their support for a recycling program.

⊃ Take a group of interested citizens with you to secure funding and support from town, city or county groups.

⊃ Decide what business structure will suit the cause best; i.e., non-profit governmental entity, etc.; if nonprofit, recruit a board.

⊃ Find an appropriate drop-off site at which the public can recycle their materials.

⊃ Secure buyers for your recycled commodities. Be clear what they will take and how they would like it; i.e., baled or loose in a box, and what they will pay per ton.

⊃ Determine the volume of goods you anticipate and how they will be shipped to the buyer.

⊃ Clearly label all bins so the public is not confused.

⊃ Advertise the grand opening with an educational project; get kids from schools involved. Make public relations, advertising and education a priority for your program—get schools and businesses involved in their own recycling programs.

⊃ Keep your site clean and free from garbage; have enough staff to monitor the site. Make it clear to the public when the site is open for collection.

- Build a material recovery facility when you have the support, volume of goods and a reliable market for all that you recycle.
- Plan for disposal of hazardous waste, and notify the community what you can take and when.

Renewable Energy

"Although there is no single technological or policy solution to climate change and energy independence in the U.S., renewable energy is clearly destined to play an important role in the years to come—and now is the time to lay the foundation."[1]

—Katie Mandes, Pew Center for Climate Change

We are coming to the end of our fossil fuel joy ride. Oil production in the United States peaked in the early 1970s. Peak oil means we explored and drilled all the locations that were financially feasible for "cheap oil," stored all that we could, and since 1970 we have been consuming more oil than we produce in the United States. We have a big appetite. "The United States consumes 19.6 million barrels per day, of oil, which is 25 percent of the world's total. As a result, the United States produces one fourth of the world's carbon emissions."[2]

When you spend more than you have in your bank account, you realize you are about to be overdrawn. The bank sends you notices and eventually you have to pay back the bank. But with our energy use, we go on borrowing from planet earth, and our debt is getting out of hand.

Unlike our personal finances, there is no loan office that can bail us out of our energy overdraft. There is no other earth on which we can take a second mortgage. Once the oil is gone, it will be gone. World Wildlife Fund Director General James Leape said, "If everyone around the world lived as those in America, we would need five planets to support us."[3]

Predictions are that our oil reserves will be gone in forty years. We can go to war to secure our access to more oil. We can cause strife in far away nations by asserting our right to profligate spending of resources, but very soon, we will need to find sustainable ways to support our lifestyles without overdrawing from the earth. The great news is that the technologies are already in place to live in a sustainable way without hardship. We could live in a comfortable way using only a quarter of the energy we do today.[4]

Energy Solutions
• • • • •

There are many possibilities for getting us out of this fossil fuel dependency.

1. Conservation is key. Amory Lovins of the Rocky Mountain Institute coined the word *negawatt*; that is, a unit of energy not spent. Some ways that we can cut our use of energy are switching to CFLs, turning off our lights, turning down our water heaters, designing our homes with passive solar and using appliances that really are efficient.

All of these solutions create negawatts that reduce our demand on the energy grid.

2. Solar energy is rapidly catching up to fossil fuels in its ability to generate a kilowatt of energy at a competitive price.

3. Wind power is a clean, renewable technology that is used much more widely in Europe, particularly in Germany and Denmark, than it is in the United States.

4. Geothermal generates 17 percent of the electricity in Iceland. We have several geothermal plants in the United States that use the earth's natural geothermal (hot water) features to generate energy. Geothermal has been used in Italy and New Zealand successfully for years. Geothermal generation plants are not to be confused with ground source heat pumps or using geothermal energy for domestic heating.

Solar Energy

We have already discussed passive solar in chapter two on green remodeling. Solar is a great solution for our homes, businesses and industries. Solar thermal, or preheating our hot water using the sun, makes sense. Installing solar thermal panels on a roof is relatively easy, and the cost of installation pays for itself in a few years. Photovoltaic (PV) panels have a longer payback period but still can generate some of your electrical needs. There are solar rebate programs, and tax incentives that can make PV solar more affordable. If you tie your system to the grid, called grid inter-tie, you can generate enough solar electricity to offset some of your electrical use. Check with your local utility for payback rates. Solar has the potential to really take off as a source of renewable energy in the United States.

Thin Film Technology

Thin film technology is the new emerging way to use the energy of the sun to power our homes, businesses and industry. The technology will be commercially available in 2008 or 2009, with many new plants coming on line around the world. The great feature of thin film is that it does not depend on silicon, which is experiencing a shortage at the moment. Demand exceeds supply for PV panels worldwide. There is not a shortage of silicon, which is sand, but a shortfall in supply of poly-silicon due to its demand as the conductive material used in manufacturing PV panels.

Thin film made by Suntech in China uses less than 2 percent of the silicon used in traditional PV panels and will end up costing about $1.20 per watt, which is significantly less expensive than current PV panels.[5] Nanosolar is another technology company to watch. Based in Palo Alto, California, and Berlin, Germany, their thin film technology uses no silicon at all. Nanosolar relies on a film of CIGS, which is copper indium gallium diselenide, to make a flexible solar fabric or film that has many different building applications. A key advantage of thin film technology is its ability to resist heat and to function on cloudy days and still generate electricity. Traditional PV panels function better at cooler temperatures. Thin film also will generate more usable power.

The cost effectiveness of solar is quite crucial to the whole renewable energy picture. If solar can become cost competitive with fossil fuels, we will be on our way to curbing our addiction to oil. Also, as solar comes on line as a viable and widely used technology, it will make it less likely that the government will subsidize nuclear power, which is not a "clean" technology. Remember that the sun is a renewable resource; it is free, clean and available to all nations rich and poor. It provides vastly more usable energy than we need. How we harness the sun's energy is up to us, but not to do so would be foolish.

Concentrating Collectors

Concentrating collectors look like a solar factory. The largest one in the world is in Kramer Junction, California. It is made up of mirrored troughs that point at the sun and concentrate sunlight that heats a transfer fluid that runs a steam generator, producing electricity. These solar "factories" must be located in sunny locations, and they require the infrastructure to carry the energy generated to the grid.

Flat Roofs

Flat roofs lend themselves to solar. Many factories, small businesses, grocery stores, warehouses and big-box stores like Wal-Mart have flat roofs. All that is needed is the funding and infrastructure to put solar technology on these roofs so they can generate their own electricity from the sun. They can also sell back to the grid whenever their need for electricity is less than the amount of electricity they are generating. When these businesses discover the financial advantages of using their roofs, they will be willing to make their own investments.

Solar-Generating Facilities

Arizona, California and Nevada are great locations for large photovoltaic arrays that generate electricity for the grid. They generally are out in the country on an unused flat piece of ground and transmit their energy from the remote site into transmission lines. There are many of these generating facilities all over the world, and we will see many more as the technology and infrastructure improve.

Wind Power

● ● ● ● ●

The Department of Energy reports that "the world's winds could theoretically supply the equivalent of 5,800 quadrillion BTUs (quads) of energy each year—more than 15 times current world energy demand. (A quad is equal to about 172 million barrels of oil, or 45 million tons of coal.)"[6] According to a study by Battelle Pacific Northwest Laboratory, "wind power could supply about 20 percent of the nation's electricity."[7] The Great Plains have been called the Saudi Arabia of wind because they have the potential to produce so much energy. North Dakota has so much wind that it could meet one-fourth of the electrical demand of the United States. Wind power is slowly coming down in its cost of generation. At the time this book is published, a kilowatt from coal is still cheaper than a kilowatt from wind, but that may change soon.

However, as with any energy source, there must be transmission lines in place to carry the electricity to its destination, and that has been the main stumbling block with wind power. Wind has also not received the kind of subsidies that nuclear has, nor has it received consistent support from Congress. Companies that are going to take the risk of making a substantial investment in wind power need to be assured that they will get the tax credits and other financial incentives that will put wind in the forefront as a renewable energy technology.

As wind becomes a more viable renewable energy, it still needs to complement other sources of energy used within a utility. If wind is about 10 percent of the mix of any given utility, then the utility can continue to meet its energy demands when the turbines are not turning. If the utility depends on the wind to meet 20 percent of its needs, problems can develop because the utility may not have alternate power sources when the wind is not blowing. So the fuel mix of any utility is important.

"The world's winds could theoretically supply... more than 15 times current world energy demand."

One concern that is often raised about wind is that the turbines are dangerous to birds and bats. The original U.S. wind farm was installed on Altamont Pass in northern California in the 1970s and had very fast-spinning rotors. While it was installed in a great spot for wind, it also happened to be a migratory bird route. Much has been learned since then. Now some of the Altamont turbines are shut down during the winter bird migration season. New turbines have bigger blades, but they turn much more slowly. Studies in Denmark on the effect of turbines on birds has determined that birds and bats can steer clear of the slower-moving turbines. Also, the old wind towers used to have perching places on them, which further endangered birds. Now the towers are taller but free of perching places, which is good for the birds.

If you are thinking of installing wind on your property, you can become part of an anemometer loan program. An anemometer measures the speed of the wind. It must be placed high on a tower and left for some time to determine if your location is possible for wind generation. Many utilities in the Great Plains states have anemometer loan programs to measure the potential for making a large investment.

The American Wind Energy Association has set an ambitious goal to produce 20 percent of America's power from wind by the year 2020.

The lack of transmission lines to areas with adequate wind is a problem but was certainly overcome for other forms of electrical generation. It will require a great deal of capitalization to bring wind up to speed, but it is a clean, renewable resource that can be a great economic development tool for small rural communities. That is more than we can say for coal, nuclear or natural gas development.

Nuclear Energy
• • • • •

In many parts of the world, with the looming threat of global warming, nuclear is being touted as the "clean energy solution." In France, 75 percent of electric power comes from nuclear plants. Nuclear power is a significant source of energy in the United States. There are currently 101 operating nuclear power plants in the United States generating about 20 percent of our energy needs. However, no new plants have been developed since 1974 because of inherent problems ranging from plant failures or accidents to disposal of spent nuclear fuel.

The lack of a secure and safe way to dispose of nuclear waste, which lasts 10,000 years, is among the most significant problems with nuclear power plants. There is currently no safe and secure facility for nuclear fuel disposal, and spent fuel is being temporarily stored in scattered facilities around the United States. Yucca Mountain in Nevada, the proposed waste facility for the United States, has been under study and development for several years. Thousands of tests have been done, hearings have been held, and yet the facility is still not determined to be safe. There may be problems with water seeping into the radioactive waste, which could then allow waste to get into the groundwater.

In addition to the problems of permanent disposal and storage of waste, the spent nuclear fuel from scattered plants and temporary facilities needs to be transported on the nation's highways and railroads through major population centers in order to reach Yucca Mountain. These transportation issues are another set of problems facing the industry. There is no apparent way at the present time to ensure that nuclear waste transportation will be safe from highway or railroad accidents or from a terrorist attack.

The lack of a secure and safe way to dispose of nuclear waste, which lasts 10,000 years, is among the most significant problems with nuclear power plants.

"The extra cost to deal with just the spent fuel that has already accumulated in the United States was estimated in 1996 by a U.S. National Academy of Sciences study as 'likely to be no less than $50 billion and easily could be over $100 billion.'"[8] Besides these huge costs, nuclear waste disposal is a very unpopular issue. One reflection of this public unhappiness is the basketball stadium in Salt Lake City, which was renamed the "Energy Solutions Arena" after being bailed out by nuclear waste companies. It has now been nicknamed the "Radium Stadium" and the "Glow Dome" by unhappy Utahns.

Although nuclear-generated electricity does not produce carbon dioxide directly, like coal-fired plants do, this "clean" technology should take into account the adverse carbon aspects of building a nuclear plant, which takes vast amounts of concrete for its huge cooling towers. The manufacture of portland cement, which is a key ingredient of concrete, produces from 6 to 8 percent of carbon dioxide worldwide.[9] Once the plant is built, there is then the remote possibility of radioactivity being emitted from the plant, which is vastly more dangerous than carbon dioxide. One of the government's arguments for weaning ourselves from fossil fuels is that our fuel supplies could be vulnerable to terrorist attacks. Presently, spent radioactive materials are sitting next to nuclear power plants awaiting approval of a disposal site. These repositories could be vulnerable to terrorist activities as well. In addition, there is the real possibility of nations producing weapons-grade plutonium as a result of their "nuclear power generation."

Another cost that is not factored into the picture of "clean" nuclear power is the extraction of uranium from the ground, a necessary ingredient for the fuel rods that produce electricity. Mining, milling, conversion and enrichment processes for uranium are highly energy intensive and can pose a health risk to miners, groundwater and downwind communities.

The last hurdle that must be crossed is that the construction of a nuclear power plant is tremendously expensive. Currently, nuclear companies are asking for large government subsidies in order to build their plants. The National Resources Defense Council calls these subsidies "a dubious commercial investment." They go on to say, "Meanwhile, these subsidies displace government funding that could otherwise be directed toward cleaner, more competitive technologies with a much wider market potential for reducing global warming pollution."[10] The newest nuclear power plant is being built in Finland and is already experiencing cost overruns. The projected total may come in at $5 billion for just one plant.

As we continue to explore truly clean technologies, while at the same time reducing the escalation of global warming, we might want to avoid the risks and financial commitments of future nuclear development.

Case Study
Farmers across the plains states have found that receiving royalties from wind turbines on their land can be more profitable than raising crops. Wind power certainly is more compatible with raising crops and ranching, than oil or gas drilling.

The Colorado Green Wind Farm project has 108 turbines, each of 1.5 MW (megawatts). They plan to send this energy to the 1.3 million customers of Xcel Energy. The Lamar, Colorado, project "spans approximately 11,840 acres owned by 14 landowners, the actual footprint of the turbine uses less than 2 percent of the total acreage. The remainder continues to be used for ranching and grazing."[11]

The Colorado Green Wind Farm is a great example of a community project that has been a win/win for everyone. Unlike communities impacted by oil and gas exploration, wind can bring positive change to a community. Many communities have experienced the pressure of oil and gas development, including the drilling of wells in residential neighborhoods. The extraction of fossil fuels can disrupt a community, create toxic waste problems, bring a drug culture to a rural environment, split the community into factions and wear out the infrastructure of a community. Wind farms, on the other hand, revitalize farm communities with good clean jobs. During construction of the wind farm in Lamar, Colorado, 400 workers were employed from around Colorado and the United States. Landowners receive $3,000 to $6,000 per turbine per year in royalties. Prowers County property tax base has increased by 29 percent, and the county has made additional revenues of

(Continued . . .)

$764,000. The school district receives $917,000 annually, the medical center $189,000, and the school bond fund $217,000.[12] This revenue is being pumped into a rural community that was withering on the vine from the demise of the family farm and several years of drought.

Action Points

• • • • •

➲ Calculate your carbon footprint by going to www.myfootprint.org. Plug in your mileage, your airplane trips and energy bills to see how many planets it takes to support your lifestyle.

➲ Once you know what your lifestyle uses, find ways that you can lessen your carbon footprint. Conserve, use public transportation and eat local and organic.

➲ See if you can get your school, business or government agency to go solar. Research rebates and incentives that are available at the state and federal levels.

➲ Explore wind as an option for your community. Sometimes the best option is offshore.

➲ Get involved in learning about nuclear power; do you want a reactor in your community? If not, what can you do about it?

➲ Find out if nuclear waste is transported through your community, either by truck or railroad. Is that safe?

- Find out if your state has a renewable energy portfolio. If it does, what kind of energy is being used? How close are they to meeting their goal?

- If your state does not have a renewable energy portfolio, see what it would take for you to get an initiative on the ballot. Some states require a certain number of signatures to launch an initiative.

- Support politicians locally, statewide and nationally who believe in renewable energy, and who are willing to support it with their votes!

CHAPTER 9

The Looking Glass

"We must no longer think of human progress as a matter of imposing ourselves on the natural environment. The world—the climate and all living things—is a closed system; what we do has consequences that eventually will come back to affect us."

—United Nations Environmental Programme[1]

As I mentioned in the introduction, it is important that we band together in our communities to find solutions to the present crisis on earth.

Changing the way we live, build, eat and drive can be a start. There are many ways to work on these topics, with your neighbors, your religious community, with a school group or at your community library. We are not in this crisis alone, and we do not have to solve it alone. Kevin Knobloch, president of Union of Concerned Scientists, says it this way: "If you want to walk fast, walk alone. If you want to walk far, walk together." He goes on to say, "It is so exciting to see scientists, doctors, members of labor unions, corporate CEOs, farmers, students, and artists—people from all vocations, income levels, and political leanings—working together to fulfill our responsibility to future generations by addressing global warming."[2]

Global Warming
• • • • •

In 1992, world leaders met in Rio de Janeiro, Brazil, to discuss the impending world crisis of greenhouse gas emissions and their warming effect on the planet. Many heartfelt speeches were made, and many scientists informed the world leaders that carbon emissions form a blanket over the earth, which traps heat in the earth's atmosphere and causes our temperatures to rise.

The group met again in Kyoto, Japan, in 1997, and 180 world leaders, except the United States and Australia, signed the Kyoto Protocol. Countries pledged to reduce their greenhouse gas emissions by a particular amount based on their 1990 levels. Each country has its target date by which its emissions will be reduced. Some countries may not meet their goal.

The Bush administration felt that the science, which was predicting global warming, might not be sound, and also that if the United States were to agree to the Kyoto Protocol, it would hurt the U.S. economy. The problem with this decision is that the United States was emitting the largest amount of greenhouse gases of any country in the world, until China surpassed it in June 2007. The worldwide movement to decrease greenhouse gas emissions has certainly been weakened by the lack of participation of the United States. Luckily, other nations around the world are taking the Kyoto Protocol seriously and doing what they can to mitigate their country's impact on global warming. Concerned officials in the United States are also taking action.

The Mayors Climate Protection Agreement
● ● ● ● ●

In 2005, Mayor Greg Nickels of Seattle saw a need for U.S. cities to enact the Kyoto Protocol since the U.S. government was immobilized by inaction. Nickels was moved to action after a particularly warm winter in the State of Washington when most of the ski areas had to close due to lack of snow. His idea is brilliant. By July 2007, 600 mayors in all fifty states representing over sixty-six million Americans have agreed to reduce the global warming impacts of their cities. Each city is approaching this agreement differently, but in general, the Mayors Climate Protection Agreement cities have pledged to enact policies and programs to meet or exceed the greenhouse gas emission reduction target recommended for the United States in the Kyoto Protocol—a 7 percent reduction from 1990 levels by 2012.

All kinds of new programs are being initiated across the country, and cities are vying to be the "greenest" city in America. There is nothing like a little competition to spur things on.

"Lincoln, Nebraska, is now running its public buses on biodiesel. Lexington, Kentucky, has replaced incandescent traffic signal bulbs with more energy efficient LED ones and added hybrid cars to its municipal fleet. In Salt Lake City, wind energy is being more widely used. Chicago awards grants for rooftop gardens that help improve air quality, conserve energy and reduce storm water runoff."[3]

The list goes on and on. Denver and Salt Lake City are expanding their light rail systems, taking thousands of cars off the highways.

Light rail reduces the carbon footprint of a city by eliminating the CO_2 exhaust from cars, and that cleans up the air of a city. Clean air doesn't just make it possible to see the mountains that have been obliterated by smog; it helps to reduce childhood and elderly asthma rates. Entire cities are changing their stoplights to light-emitting diodes (LEDs), which save thousands of dollars by using less energy. Many cities are mandating that all of their public buildings be built according to LEED standards. By passing these regulations, the cities are proving that they can make a difference. When public buildings are nontoxic, built to last, have lovely green spaces inside, and are lit with daylight, it sends a strong message to the public that green building makes sense.

ICLEI
● ● ● ● ●

The International Council for Local Environmental Initiatives (ICLEI) is an offshoot of the United Nations and helps local governments with technical consulting and support for local programs in sustainability. One of their programs is the Cities for Climate Protection (CCP), which will help your city figure out how to reduce its greenhouse gases, and address emissions and their impact on air quality. CCP works all over the world and has expertise that might not be available in your town or county. They will help your town or city analyze how their municipal decisions affect global warming. For example, your town or city may have a fleet of vehicles, police cars, water district trucks, maintenance trucks or buses, all running on various fuels with a range of fuel efficiency. It is possible to coordinate the fuel efficiencies of a city fleet to reduce the amount the city is spending on fuel, and ultimately to reduce your city's greenhouse gas emissions. Some cities provide a collection of bicycles to city employees to use to get to and from meetings, without having to drive a city vehicle. It is great for cities and towns to set examples for their population about how to get out of their cars, reduce their emissions and live a more sustainable lifestyle. There is a ripple effect from our local governments into the private sector businesses and into our households that truly will make a difference. Presently, CCP has 680 participating cities in thirty-one countries, from Alachua County, Florida, to Woolahra, Australia.[4]

The 2030 Challenge
• • • • •

Architect Ed Mazria has put forth a challenge to the building community to reduce the amount of energy buildings use. He suggests that all buildings be carbon neutral by the year 2030. A carbon neutral building uses no external source of energy but generates it all on-site. Some skyscrapers are going carbon neutral. Some residences, businesses and schools are as well. Mazria outlines how this can be done, incrementally. It has to do with the design of buildings, what materials are chosen, how buildings are insulated for efficient heating and cooling and the use of renewable energy.

Mazria was the author of the *Passive Solar House Book* in the 1970s, so he understands energy and he is quite familiar with the architecture and design communities. In January 2007, he held a teach-in linked by satellite, which brought together designers, architects and students from around the world. He presented his ideas along with several other dynamic speakers, and in the end, he asked design schools, architecture firms, businesses and municipalities to agree to meet the 2030 Challenge. It begins with designing a building to use 50 percent less energy than a similar building in the same community. If a hospital is being designed, it must use 50 percent less energy than an existing hospital in the same region. It's the same with schools, office buildings and government buildings.

The building sector is the largest contributor to greenhouse gases because of the amount of energy that goes into manufacturing materials, and energy spent heating and cooling buildings.

Mazria has upped the ante. It may not be enough for a building to meet basic LEED standards. Although a LEED building will be far superior to a noncertified building, it may not meet the 50 percent energy reduction. The building sector is the largest contributor to greenhouse gases due to the amount of energy that goes into manufacturing materials, and energy spent heating and cooling buildings.

We can be hopeful that the 2030 Challenge will wake up the architecture and design communities to do their part to curb global warming.

Triple Bottom Line

• • • • •

Many businesses are starting to consider more than their net profits. The triple bottom line takes the environmental and social justice practices of a company into account. For example, if a company is turning quite a profit but creating environmental damage in the course of manufacturing, that environmental damage has a cost. Society and possibly the company will have to pay for this damage at some point. If a business cleans up its environmental record, it often does better financially. At the same time, if employees are treated equitably, and paid a fair wage, the productivity of a company will increase. These three aspects of business must be part of all business practices of the future.

Green Roofs
• • • • •

Green roofs are one of the many ways cities are reducing the amount of greenhouse gases they produce. Plants clean the air and act as air filters for emissions from cars and buildings. By planting the flat roofs on many buildings, a city can improve its air quality.

The green roof on city hall in Chicago recorded a temperature of 90 degrees during its first summer. The roof next door, which is not green, recorded a temperature of 170 degrees.

Mayor Richard M. Daley of Chicago installed a green roof on city hall in 2001 to test the technology of green roofs and to set an example. The wonderful thing about green roofs in cities is that they cool down the city. The green roof on city hall in Chicago recorded a maximum temperature of 90 degrees during its first summer. The roof next door, which is not green, recorded a temperature of 170 degrees.[5] The city hall's green roof is visible from many surrounding buildings, offering visual respite in an otherwise grey, concrete landscape. The flowers and grasses atop the city hall serve as habitat for birds and insects. Because the roof is thicker than a normal roof, it provides extra heating and cooling effects for the building, holding the heat in during winter, and keeping the heat out in the summer.

A green roof also extends the life of a roof membrane by not exposing it to solar radiation. Another great feature is that it captures rainwater and does not send runoff to the storm drains. In a large city with overloaded storm drains, this can be a significant bonus. The pilot project on Chicago's city hall has been a great success, drawing attention from around the country and encouraging other green roofs to be built.

Soon there will be over one million square feet of green roofs within the city limits of Chicago. As this green landscape grows, it may bring back a vitality of wildlife that has been driven away by the concrete jungle.

The city hall in Chicago has a team of naturalists that monitor the different species of birds and insects living on the green roof. They have also put beehives on the roof that are attracting native bees back to Chicago.

Green Skyscrapers

As part of the effort to green our cities, many buildings are being built either as LEED buildings or buildings that incorporate green design ideas. Some green skyscrapers generate all of their own energy, even selling excess back to the grid. The new Bank of America building at One Bryant Park in New York City will have fuel cells in the basement generating the building's electricity from natural gas. Some buildings have been designed with wind turbines to generate energy, and other tall buildings make use of wind-generated convection currents to cool offices at night and exchange the stale air from the workday. Many office buildings are realizing that workers like operable windows or at least the ability to control fresh-air intake at their workstations.

Lighting and computers can be designed to be motion activated, so electricity is not wasted; waterless urinals and timed faucets in bathrooms conserve water; and solar panels or film on the outside of tall buildings generate electricity without taxing the grid.

Recycling is a planned part of new urban buildings instead of being an afterthought.

Many new buildings have collection facilities for office paper, printer cartridges and cans and bottles built into their supply closets. This makes recycling part of the workday, done systematically by all employees rather than just a few.

Traffic Congestion Taxes

● ● ● ● ●

I objected to the name of Al Gore's film, *An Inconvenient Truth*, at first, because if people feel they will be inconvenienced, they are less likely to change. But it would be really inconvenient if New York City and London were underwater. If we do not stem global warming, it is possible that the melting glaciers, particularly in Greenland, could cause a rise of twenty-three feet in the oceans. This would happen over the course of many years, but New York and London are not taking any chances.

Mayor Michael Bloomberg of New York proposed a congestion tax for downtown Manhattan of $8 for cars and $21 for trucks. Stiffly opposed by many, the mayor's plan is now garnering support from 141 different groups and organizations, including the teamsters. The truck drivers will get a discount if they upgrade their trucks. The fee will be reduced from $21 to $7 if a trucker can prove that their diesel engine is now energy efficient, or that they have upgraded to reduce their emissions. New York taxis, exempt from the tax, have also been offered incentives if they switch to hybrid taxis.

There are those who complain that the tax will hurt the middle- and low-income workers who commute into New York, but very few workers come into the city by car. Many New Yorkers cannot afford the insurance and parking fees to keep a car in the city anyway. Even the mayor rides the train to work.

The plan, if passed by the state legislature in Albany, will generate revenues of close to $400 million a year, which will be used to upgrade the city's transportation system. If the plan goes through, New York could reduce its CO_2 emissions by a projected 30 percent. Mayor Bloomberg calls this "the most dramatic reduction in greenhouse gases ever achieved by any American city."[6]

Congestion taxes not only curb carbon emissions, they make it possible for commerce to take place more efficiently. Workers who are caught in maddening traffic don't get their jobs done, delivery trucks can't deliver when they are sitting still and commerce that must use trucks needs to be able to complete as many transactions as possible to keep their business profitable. Time is money, as we all know.

London instituted a congestion tax in 2003, which has reduced the traffic in the central city by 30 percent. The tax is only imposed during business hours, which allows weekend business and theater-goers to travel to the city center tax free. Mayor Ken Livingstone has extended the congestion tax into a district beyond downtown, and even got reelected.

Financial Consequences of Non-Action

• • • • •

Sir Nicholas Stern of London has written the most extensive report on global warming to date. The most striking part of his report is the projected economic consequences of ignoring global warming. Stern is head of the Government Economics Service and is the advisor to the British government of the economics of climate change. The Stern Report says even if we act now, extreme weather could cause a 1 percent reduction of the global gross domestic product, but we may have a chance of stemming the tide. If we completely ignore global warming, the consequences could reduce our gross domestic product by as much as 20 percent in the worst-case scenario. Imagine losing 20 percent of your hard-earned income. What would that mean to you and your family? If we make the changes in our lifestyles now, we may be able to avert the crisis. The mayors of New York and London are doing their part. There are other ways to be creative that offer promise for the future.

Biomimicry

We have the ability to learn from nature, but most of us have lost our connection with the earth. We may go for a hike or ride our bike, but the realization that nature has a great depth of intelligence may have escaped us. Biomimicry looks at the way nature behaves, and from that study, has learned ways to design things more efficiently. Nature does not waste energy, nor create large refuse dumps the way humans do. By studying nature, new products have been designed that can help us find solutions.

For example, by studying the way a whale's flipper is designed, we may be able to shape aircraft wings and helicopter rotors to be more efficient, and therefore use less fuel.

"Humpback whale flippers are scalloped with prominent knobs called a tubercles."[7] When tested in the laboratory, scalloped flippers were found to have less drag, more lift and the ability to withstand a stall better than a straight flipper. If this information can be extrapolated and applied to airplane wings, we may be able to design a better way of flying that does not use so much fuel.

By mimicking termite tunnels and pathways of air currents, architects have been able to build an office building that requires no air conditioning in a very hot climate.

Another brilliant example of biomimicry is the design of buildings that mimic termite mounds. In Zimbabwe, architects have studied the constant temperature of termite mounds to figure out how they cool themselves even though the outside temperature fluctuates widely and becomes extremely hot during the day. By mimicking termite tunnels and pathways of air currents, architects have been able to build an office building called Eastgate that requires no air conditioning in a very hot climate. "By studying termite mounds, the project team discovered a natural form of air-conditioning. During the day, the tops of the mounds are warmed by the sun, and at night the warm tops create suction, drawing cool air in at the base. Eastgate mimics this system . . . the air chills the concrete slabs under the office floors and keeps the interior comfortable during the day"[8] The building uses less electricity than surrounding buildings because it is daylit and also has no air conditioning. The builders saved $3.5 million by not having to import an air conditioning plant. Rents are 20 percent lower in the building because the energy savings are passed to the customers.

Biomimicry teaches us more than nature's ways, it teaches us humility. Man has always envisioned himself at the top of the heap. Nature has been considered for its potential to serve our desire for consumption and domination. By noticing how certain species survive, what they take from nature and what they give back, we can learn to live more harmoniously with nature.

When we design buildings, highways, products and packaging with nature in mind, we begin to see ourselves as just a small part of the entire earthly dance. We can practice ethical biomimicry without extracting from or altering nature. If we take a flounder gene, insert it in a tomato so the tomato will resist cold and ship better, we are modifying instead of mimicking. If we design alfalfa seed with pesticide implanted, and spray fields to kill weeds without harming the alfalfa, we are changing nature, which could harm the planet and ourselves.

Future of Food

● ● ● ● ●

My looking glass is a bit clouded when it comes to food. It is very hard to predict what will happen with genetically modified (GM) food in America. If Monsanto prevails, most of our conventional food will have been genetically modified in some way. Presently, about two-thirds of all processed food in America has been genetically modified. GM crops are supposedly pest resistant, but after a period of years, superweeds begin to appear, and then even more toxic pesticides must be applied to our food. Many countries have bans on GM food or require that it be labeled. It is important that we find local, non-GM sources for our food, rather than buy food that may be healthy, but has been shipped a long distance. As people become aware of the amount of fossil fuel it takes to raise beef cattle, they may choose to eat lower on the food chain. Untainted fish may disappear altogether. If communities want healthier food, they will need to find a way to get it.

Presently about two-thirds of all processed food in America has been genetically modified. GM crops are supposedly pest resistant, but after a period of years, superweeds begin to appear, and then even more toxic pesticides must be applied to our food.

Getting Involved
● ● ● ● ●

In the future, we will see more involvement. A vast, grassroots movement is building around the world. Each of us is a part of it. Let this be a jumping-off point to launch you into starting your own community programs, writing your own books, running for office in your community or changing the way things are done. Al Gore, The Stern Report and the Intergovernmental Panel on Climate Change say that if we continue with business as usual, we will experience the consequences of global warming adversely impacting all nations and most particularly the poorer nations. Some experts say that we only have a short time to turn around the deterioration caused by our constant emissions that are warming the planet.

Now is the time to initiate change.

CHAPTER 10

The Long View

"Let ours be a time remembered for the awakening of a new reverence for life, the firm resolve to achieve sustainability, the quickening struggle for justice and peace, and the joyful celebration of life."[1]

—The Earth Charter

While driving home last night listening to music by Corelli, I was struck by all the different instruments that it takes to make such beautiful and complex music. Multiple tones, harmonies, chords and rhythms were woven together to create a work of art. I remember Bobby McFerrin's Voicestra, a gathering together of voices for harmony, beauty and playfulness. Wouldn't it be amazing if all of our voices could find a harmony together to bring peace and joy to this earth?

After September 11, there was potential for a world community to emerge, not out of fear, but by hearts blown open by a shared tragedy. But people often react impulsively out of grief or fear, and we were led in the direction of retaliation at great cost to the world. The American public has expressed its outrage at the war in Iraq and the loss of 3,707 of our young people as well as the expense of $2 billion a week. The true cost of lives, unstable governments, civil war and total disruption of countries can never be tabulated. There is only one way to repair the damage, and that is with the capacity of the human heart.

As the infrastructure of America crumbles, we human beings have to become the new infrastructure. Our hearts and minds will be the new strength, but instead of using that strength to fight a perceived enemy, we must use it to form a community of the heart.

There is an ancient figure named Avaloketesvara that has four arms and a thousand hands. This one being represents the capacity for infinite compassion, with the thousand hands able to embrace all suffering and all beings. We each have at least a thousand hands and the same abilities. They may be buried deep inside us, as precious jewels are buried in the earth.

The Industrial Revolution has mined a good part of the world's resources, digging minerals and metals from the ground to fuel our voracious appetite for growth and material wealth. As I said earlier, it takes five planets to support our lifestyle in America.

But this can change, as we each mine the capacity of the human heart. Most of us in developed nations have enough material goods, food, shelter and the ability to work, and yet we want more.

I think this longing for things can be replaced with a longing for connection, for peace, for friendship. As the poet Rumi says, "There are a thousand ways to kneel down and kiss the earth." Each of us will find our way. As the heart informs us what our next action will be, we begin to walk the path of wisdom and compassion.

A teacher of mine, Jack Kornfield, says, "There is no grief too big for the heart to hold." Some are saddened by America's declining position among industrialized nations. We rank thirty-seventh in healthcare, we are the second worst in infant mortality rates and our infrastructure doesn't support us as well as it used to. We can embrace the earth community, which offers us more solace and inner wealth than the material world ever could.

It is time for the long view. Looking into the future, we begin to understand the cyclical nature of things, and from that view can temper our immediate need as consumers.

This crisis is driving us into new opportunities to leave behind the false security of nationalism and gated communities for a world of relationships and openness.

This is not to say we can sit back and relax. There are those who call for a "warlike" effort to fight global warming. I prefer the peaceful images of women planting trees in Kenya, children teaching their parents to recycle, of species teaching humans how to move through the world with efficiency and families building their houses from the earth.

Just as President John F. Kennedy was able to inspire engineering firms and factories to put a man on the moon, we, as inventive and creative people, ought to be able to put our hearts and minds together to solve this global warming crisis.

In the Chinese book of changes called the *I Ching*, the symbol for crisis is related to the symbol of opportunity. This crisis is driving us into new opportunities to leave behind the false security of nationalism and gated communities for a world of relationships and openness. We need to get to know our neighbors, to trade in our arrogance and insecurity, and cultivate humility, generosity and compassion for all who inhabit this fragile earth. As competition gives way to collaboration, companies share their trade secrets to solve problems, nations forgive national debts; peoples around the world will celebrate our diversity for the richness it offers.

We are not alone and we will go forward together into the unknown, kissing the earth and each other.

Notes

Chapter 1: Save Energy, Save Money

1. Dalai Lama, *The Heart of Compassion* (Twin Lakes, WI: Lotus Press, 2002).

2. http://www.architecture2030.org/current_situation/current5.html, n.d.

3. Paul Scheckel, *Home Energy Diet* (Gabriola Island, BC, Canada: New Society Publishers, 2005).

Chapter 2: Remodel Green: Here Comes the Sun

1. Ed Mazria, "The 2010 Imperative," http://www.architecture2030.org/2010_imperative/index, n.d.

2. Paula Baker-LaPorte and others, *Prescriptions for a Healthy House* (Gabriola Island, BC, Canada: New Society Publishers, 2001), 175.

3. "The Wingspread Version of the Precautionary Principle," http://www.sehn.org/wing.html, n.d.

4. David Johnston and Kim Master, *Remodeling Green*, (Gabriola Island, BC, Canada: New Society Publishers, 2004).

5. Ibid.

6. http://www.tanklesswaterheaters.com, n.d.

7. "Saving Electricity: Washing Machines," http://www.michaelbluejay.com/electricity/laundry, n.d.

8. Michael Grower and Warren Leon, *The Consumers Guide to Effective Environmental Choices* (New York: Three Rivers Press, 1999), 68.

9. Jason Daley and Florence Williams, *Outside Magazine*, April 2007.

10. David Johnston and Kim Master, *Remodeling Green* (Gabriola Island, BC, Canada: New Society Press, 2004).

Chapter 3: Green Building

1. *Building with Vision* (Healdsburg, CA: Watershed Media, Inc., 2001).

2. John Ritter, *USA Today*, July 26, 2006.

3. Alex Wilson, *Your Green Home* (Gabriola Island, BC, Canada: New Society Publishers, 2006).

4. *Building with Vision* (Healdsburg, CA: Watershed Media, Inc., 2001).

5. Clarke Snell and Tim Callahan, *Green Building: A Complete How-To Guide to Alternative Building Methods* (New York: Lark Books, 2005).

Chapter 4: Green Schools and Hospitals

1. The City of Stockton, California, *Energy Efficiency Schools, High Performance Schools*, http://www.stocktongov.com/energysaving/schools/performanceschools.cfm, n.d.

2. http://www.h-m-g.com/projects/daylighting/summaries%20on%20daylighting.htm, n.d.

3. *A Summary of Studies Related to Student Health and Productivity*, Massachusetts Technology Collaborative, Renewable Energy Trust, http://www.mtpc.org/Project%20Deliverables/GB_General_LIFT.pdf, n.d.

4. *Healthier, Wealthier and Wiser*, Global Green USA's Green Schools Report, http://www.globalgreen.org/media/greenbuilding/GG_Green_School_Report.pdf, n.d.

5. http://www.epa.gov/iaq/pubs/insidest.html, n.d.

6. http://www.halexandria.org/dward048.htm, n.d.

7. Hospitals for a Healthy Environment, http://www.h2e-online.org/docs/h2e10stepgreenclean-r5.pdf. n.d.

8. Melissa Gaskill, "Going Green: RNs Tackle Hospital Waste," *Nurse Week*, April 24, 2006.

9. Ibid.

10. Jim Grimm, *Seattle Daily Journal of Commerce*, November 18, 2004.

Chapter 5: Cars, Trains, and Planes: Energy Solutions

1. http://www.environmentaldefense.org/documents/5301_Globalwarmingontheroad.pdf, n.d.

2. http://terrapass.com, n.d.

3. http://www.environmentaldefense.org/documents/5301_Globalwarmingontheroad.pdf, n.d.

4. David Freeman, *Winning Our Energy Independence* (Layton, Utah: Gibbs Smith, Publisher, 2007) 179.

5. http://gov.ca.gov/index.php?/print-version/press-release/6485/, n.d.

6. http://www.calcars.org, n.d.

7. http://www.hymotion.com, n.d.

8. www.solarelectricvehicles.com, n.d.

9. David Freeman, *Winning our Energy Independence* (Layton, Utah: Gibbs Smith, Publisher, 2007), 133.

10. Mark Z. Jacobson, http://news-service.stanford.edu/pr/2007/pr-ethanol-041807.html, n.d.

11. http://www.ecy.wa.gov/news/2005news/2005-251.html, http://www.shurepower.com, n.d.

12. http://www.idleaire.com, n.d.

13. http://news.bbc.co.uk/1/hi/business/6203636.stm, n.d.

14. Geoffrey B. Holland and James J. Provenzano, *The Hydrogen Age: Empowering A Clean-Energy Future* (Layton, Utah: Gibbs Smith, Publisher, 2007), 271.

Chapter 6: Local, Organic, Sustainable Food

1. John Ikerd, "Intelligent Food Economics," *Touch the Soil*, May/June 2007, 36.

2. Barbara Kingsolver and others, *Animal, Vegetable, Miracle . . . A Year of Food Life* (New York, New York: Harper Collins Publishers, 2007), 5.

3. Rich Pirog and others, "Food, Fuel and Freeways," http://www.leopold.iastate.edu/pubs/staff/ppp/food_mil.pdf, n.d.

4. http://www.urbanext.uiuc.edu/veggies/lettuce1.html, n.d.

5. http://www.sustainabletable.org/blog/archives/2007/02/small_farm_numb.html, n.d.

6. http://www.marinorganic.org, n.d.

7. http://www.localharvest.org/csa.jsp, n.d.

8. Andrew Martin, *How to Add Oomph to 'Organic,'* New York Times, Sunday, August 19, 2007.

Chapter 7: Save Water, Recycle

1. http://clima.casaccia.enea.it/ipcc/focalpoint/infoclima/2006/Europa.pdf, n.d.

2. Tim Appenzeller, "The Big Thaw," *National Geographic*, June 2007, 58.

3. http://www.sciencedaily.com/releases/2007/06/070605120933.htm, n.d.

4. Dennis Cauchon, "Lake Superior: The World's Largest Freshwater Lake . . ." *USA Today*, June 13, 2007.

5. http://en.wikipedia.org/wiki/Mobro_4000, n.d.

Chapter 8: Renewable Energy

1. Katie Mandes, "The Expanding Role of State Renewable Energy Policy," The Pew Center for Climate Change, http://www.pewclimate.org/press_room/sub_press_room/2006_releases/rps_release.cfm, n.d.

2. http://maps.unomaha.edu/Peterson/funda/sidebar/OilConsumption.html, n.d.

3. http://www.msnbc.msn.com/id/15398149, n.d.

4. *Crude Impact*, film by James Jandak Wood, Independent Documentary by Vista Clara Films.

5. http://www.insidegreentech.com/node/1208, n.d.

6. http://www.solarwindhydro.com, n.d.

7. http://www.solarwindhydro.com, n.d.

8. Beth Wellington, "Law and Technology Resources," February 12, 2007, www.llrx.com/extras/nuclearenergy.htm, n.d.

9. http://www.us-concrete.com/news/features.asp, n.d.

10. http://www.nrdc.org/policy, n.d.

11. http://www.ppmenergy.com/rel_03.10.27.html, n.d.

12. Clipper Windpower, http://www.eesi.org/briefings/2006/NonEESI Events/RackstrawPresentation.pdf, n.d.

Chapter 9: The Looking Glass

1. United Nations Environmental Programme.

2. Union of Concerned Scientists, *Earthwise*, 9, no. 3 (summer 2007).

3. http://www.iht.com/articles/2006/10/23/business/kyoto.php, n.d.

4. http://www.iclei.org/index.php?id=800 (accessed June 19, 2007).

5. Katherine Millet, "Birds on a Cool Green Roof," *Chicago Wilderness Magazine*, summer 2004.

6. Elizabeth Kolbert, "Don't Drive, He Said," The New Yorker, May 7, 2007.

7. http://www.biomimicry.net/casestudywhalefin.htm (accessed June 19, 2007).

8. David Gissen, ed., *Big and Green, Toward Sustainable Architecture in the 21st Century* (New York: Princeton Architectural Press; Washington, D.C.: National Building Museum), 62.

Chapter 10: The Long View

1. http://www.earthcharterusa.org/earth-charter.html (accessed 6/20/07).

Resources

Architecture

Web Sites and Organizations

The 2030 Challenge
Global architecture and building
community to reduce energy use.
www.architecture2030.org/home.html

The Biomimicry Institute
www.biomimicryinstitute.org

GreenSource: The Magazine of Sustainable Design
www.greensourcemag.com

McDonough Braungart Design
Chemistry, LLC
Consultancy focused on helping
clients implement Cradle-to-Cradle
Design, a positive new approach to
sustainability and prosperity.
www.mbdc.com

National Building Museum
401 F Street NW
Washington, D.C. 20001
202-272-2448
www.nbm.org

Rate it Green
Resource sharing on products and information.
www.rateitgreen.com

Sustainable Green Pages
Northeast Sustainable Energy Association
50 Miles Street
Greenfield, MA 01301
413-774-6051
www.nesea.org/syp

Green Architects

Architect directory in the
Green Home Guide
www.greenhomeguide.com/index.php
/service/C183

Books

David Gissen, ed., *Big & Green:
Toward Sustainable Architecture in
the 21st Century* (New York, NY:
Princeton Architectural Press;
Washington, D.C.: National
Building Museum, 2002).

Paula Baker-Laporte and others,
*Prescriptions for A Healthy House,
a Practical Guide for Architects,
Builders & Homeowners* (British
Columbia, Canada: New Society
Publishers, 2001).

Paula Baker-Laporte and Robert
Laporte, *EcoNest: Creating
Sustainable Sanctuaries of Clay,
Straw, and Timber* (Layton, UT:
Gibbs Smith, Publisher, 2005).

Janine M. Benyus, *Biomimicry:
Innovation Inspired by Nature* (New
York, NY: Harper Collins, 1997).

Jennifer Roberts, *Good Green
Kitchens: The Ultimate Resource for
Creating a Beautiful, Healthy, Eco-
Friendly Kitchen* (Layton, UT:
Gibbs Smith, Publisher, 2006).

William McDonough and Michael
Braungart, *Cradle to Cradle:
Remaking the Way We Make
Things* (New York, NY: North
Point Press, 2002).

Building and Home/Business Improvement

Web sites and Organizations

www.buildinggreen.com

www.builditgreen.org

www.conservationcenter.org

www.ecobuilding.org

www.efficientwindows.org

Energy Star for New Homes:
www.energystar.gov/index.cfm?c=new
_homes.hm_index
www.energy.gov/buildings
www.epa.gov/iaq/greenbuilding

Environmental Building News
A newsletter.
www.buildinggreen.com

Green Building Blocks
Resource for green-building supplies,
green-building techniques and
business promotion.
www.greenbuildingblocks.com/index.go

Green Building Festivals
www.westcoastgreen.com

Green Your Home
www.greenhome.com

Greener Buildings
Resource center for environmentally
responsible building development.
www.greenerbuildings.com

GreenSeal
A nonprofit dedicated to promoting
environmentally sustainable products
and practices.
www.greenseal.org

Healthy Building Network
Advocating environmental health and
justice in homes and workplaces.
www.healthbuilding.net

Healthy House Institute
www.healthyhouseinstitute.com

Homes Across America
A showcase of resource-efficient homes.
www.homes-across-america.org

Office of Energy Efficiency, Canada
Articles and fact sheets on home
building and renovations.
http://oee.nrcan.gc.ca/publications

Scientific Certification Systems
Certifies environmentally preferred
products.
www.scscertified.com

U.S. Green Building Council
LEED, Leadership in Energy and
Environmental Design.
www.usgbc.org

Green Building Supply Stores

Bettencourt Green Building Supplies
70 N. 6th St.
Brooklyn, NY 11211
718-218-6737
www.bettencourtwood.com

Building for Health Materials Center
102 Main St.
Carbondale, CO 81623
800-292-4838
www.buildingforhealth.com

Build It Green! NYC
Salvage surplus and low-cost
building materials.
3-17 – 26th Ave. at 4th St.
Astoria, NY 11102
718-777-0132
www.bignyc.org

Directory by State
www.naturalhomemagazine.com/
buy-green.html

Eco-Green Living
1469 Church St. NW
Washington, D.C. 20005
202-234-7110
www.Eco-GreenLiving.com

ECO-WISE
110 W. Elizabeth
Austin, TX 78704
512-326-4474
www.ecowise.com

Environmental Building Supplies
819 SE Taylor St.
Portland, OR 97214
503-222-3881
www.ecohaus.com

Environmental Home Center
4121 First Ave. S.
Seattle, WA 98134
800-281-9785
www.environmentalhomecenter.com

Fairfax Hardware and Lumber
109 Broadway
Fairfax, CA 94930
415-453-4410
www.fairfaxlumber.com

Goodman Building Supply
775 Redwood Hwy.
Mill Valley, CA 94941
415-388-6233

Green Building Center
1952 E. 2700 S.
Salt Lake City, UT 84106
801-484-6278
www.greenbuildingcenter.net

Green Fusion Design Center
14 Greenfield Ave.
San Anselmo, CA
415-454-0174
www.greenfusiondesigncenter.com

Greenmaker Building Supply
2500 N. Pulaski Rd.
Chicago, IL 60639
773-384-7500
www.greenmakersupply.com

GreenWorks Building Supply
386 W. 8th Ave.
Vancouver, British Columbia, Canada
604-685-3611
www.GreenworksBuildingSupply.com

Habitat for Humanity Restore
Retail outlets selling used and surplus
building materials at a fraction of
normal prices.
www.habitat.org/env/restores.aspx

The Healthiest Home
135 Holland Ave.
Ottawa, Ontario, Canada
613-715-9014
www.TheHealthiestHome.com

Living Green
180 Center St.
Jackson, WY 83001
307-733-2152

Maine Green Building Supply
111 Fox St.
Portland, ME 04101
207-780-1500
www.maingreenbuilding.com

NEXUS Green Building
Resource Center
Resources, samples and a library.
38 Chauncy St., 7th Fl.
Boston, MA 02111
www.nexusboston.com

Refuge Sustainable Building Center
714 E Mendenhall St.
Bozeman, MT 59715
406-585-9958
www.refugebuilding.com

Straw, Sticks and Bricks
115 W. 18th St.
Kansas City, MO 6410
816-421-7171
www.strawsticksandbricks.com

Books

Alastair Fuad-Luke, *EcoDesign: The Sourcebook* (San Francisco: Chronicle Books, 2002).

Alex Wilson and Mark Piepkorn, eds., *Green Building Products: The GreenSpec Guide to Residential Building Materials* (Brattleboro, VT: Building Green; Gabriola Island, BC, Canada: New Society Publishers, 2005).

Alex Wilson, *Your Green Home: A Guide to Planning a Healthy, Environmentally Friendly New Home* (Gabriola Island, BC, Canada: New Society Publishers, 2006).

Athena Swentzell Steen, Bill Steen and others, *The Straw Bale House* (White River Junction, VT: Chelsea Green Publishing Company, 1994).

Clarke Snell and Tim Callahan, *Building Green: A Complete How-To Guide to Alternative Building Methods* (Asheville, NC: Lark Books, 2005).

Daniel D. Chiras, *The New Ecological Home: A Complete Guide to Green Building Options* (White River Junction, VT: Chelsea Green Publishing Company, 2004).

Daniel D. Chiras, *The Solar House: Passive Heating and Cooling* (White River Junction, VT: Chelsea Green Publishing Company, 2002).

Dan Imhoff, *Building with Vision: Optimizing and Finding Alternatives to Wood* (Healdsburg, CA: Watershed Media, 2001).

Dan Phillips, *Designs for a Healthy Home: An Eco-Friendly Approach* (San Francisco: SOMA Books, 2002).

David Johnston and Kim Master, *Green Remodeling: Changing the World One Room at a Time* (Gabriola Island, BC, Canada: New Society Publishers, 2004).

James Kachadorian, *The Passive Solar House: Using Solar Design to Heat & Cool Your Home* (White River Junction, VT: Chelsea Green Publishing Company, 1997).

Jennifer Roberts, *Good Green Homes: Creating Better Homes for a Healthier Planet* (Layton, UT: Gibbs Smith, Publisher, 2003).

John Schaeffer and Doug Pratt, eds., *Real Goods Solar Living Source Book* (Hopland, CA: Gaiam Real Goods, 2001).

Joseph Lstiburek, *Builder's Guide to Cold Climates: Details for Design and Construction* (Newton, CT: Taunton Press, Inc., 2000).

Sarah Susanka, *The Not So Big House: A Blueprint for the Way We Really Live* (Newtown, CT: Taunton Press, 1998).

Building Products

Web Sites and Organizations

ALTERNATIVE ENERGY

Real Goods
Green and solar living products.
www.realgoods.com

APPLIANCES

Asko
Washers, dryers and dishwashers.
www.askoUSA.com

Bosch
Washers, dryers, ranges, dishwashers.
www.boschappliances.com

Find the most energy-efficient
appliances:
www.aceee.org

Maytag
Refrigerators and laundry equipment.
www.maytag.com

BEDS, BEDDING AND MATTRESSES

Coyuchi
Organic cotton sheets and towels.
www.coyuchiorganic.com

Earthsake
Natural bedding and mattresses.
www.earthsake.com

Green Sleep
Cotton and wool mattresses.
www.greensleep.com

Heart of Vermont
Organic bedding and futons.
www.heartofvermont.com

High Desert Naturals
Home furnishings.
www.hdndesigns.com

Lifekind
Organic mattresses and bedding.
www.lifekind.com

Native Organic Cotton
Organic bedding and towels.
www.nativeorganic.com

Savvy Rest
Organic mattresses and pillows.
www.savvyrest.com

Shepherd's Dream
Wool bedding and mattresses.
www.shepherdsdream.com

BATHROOM FIXTURES

Caroma USA
Dual-flush toilet.
www.caromaUSA.com

Kohler
Low-flow, dual-flush toilets.
www.kohler.com

Toto USA
Dual-flush toilets.
www.totoUSA.com

BUILDING MATERIALS

Agriboard Industries
Renewable resources transformed into
insulated panels.
www.agriboard.com

Bonded Logic
Recycled denim insulation.
www.bondedlogic.com

Certified Forest Products
Formaldehyde-free lumber.
www.certifiedforestproducts.com

Columbia Forest Products
www.columbiaforestproducts.com

Durisol Wall Form System
Insulated concrete forming system.
www.durisolbuild.com

EcoStar
Recycled rubber and roof tiles.
www.ecostarinc.com

EcoTimber
Forest Stewardship Council flooring
and decking.
www.ecotimber.com

James Hardie
Fiber-cement siding.
www.jameshardie.com

Perform Wall
Insulated concrete forms.
www.performwall.com

Structural Insulated Panel Association
www.sips.org

Trex
Composite decking with recycled
content.
www.trex.com

Weyerhauser-ChoiceDek
Recycled material decking.
www.choicedek.com

CABINETS

Berkeley Mills
FSC custom cabinets.
www.berkeleymills.com

Neil Kelly
Formaldehyde-free cabinets.
www.neilkellycabinets.com

CARPETS AND RUGS

Carpet America Recovery Effort
www.carpetrecovery.org

Earth Weave Carpet Mills, Inc.
Renewable floor coverings.
www.earthweave.com

Henricksen Naturlich
Sustainable flooring and carpet.
www.naturalfloors.net

InterfaceFlor
Recycled carpet tiles.
www.interfaceflor.com

Nature's Carpet
Biodegradable carpet.
www.naturescarpet.com

New Moon Rugs
Chemical-free wool rugs.
www.newmoonrugs.com

Shaw Contract Group
Sustainable carpet.
www.shawcontractgroup.com

Shaw Innovation
Recyclable carpet.
www.ecoworx.com

CLEANING PRODUCTS

Begleys Best
All-natural cleaner.
www.begleysbest.com

Biokleen
Natural and nontoxic cleaners.
www.biokleenhome.com

Dr. Bronner's Magic Soap
Organic soap products.
www.drbronner.com

Earth Friendly Products
Plant-based cleaners.
www.ecos.com

Ecover
Dishwashing, laundry and
household cleaners.
www.ecover.com/us

Lifekind Naturally Safer
Natural cleaning products.
www.lifekind.com

Seaside Naturals
Natural cleaning products.
www.seasidenaturals.com

Seventh Generation
Nontoxic cleaning products.
www.seventhgeneration.com

COUNTERTOPS

Counter Production
Recycle-glass and mineral surface.
www.counterproduction.com

Kliptech/Paperstone
Recycle-paper composite.
www.kliptech.com

Oceanside Glasstile
Recycled glass tile.
www.glasstiles.com

Richlite
Recycled paper and non-toxic resin.
www.richlite.com

Sandhill Industries
One hundred percent
recycled glass tiles.
www.sandhillind.com

ShetkaStone
Recycled paper countertops.
www.shetkastone.com

Squak Mountain Stone
Natural stone alternative.
www.tmi-online.com

Totally Bamboo
Bamboo countertops.
www.totallybamboo.com

FABRIC AND UPHOLSTERY

Designtex
PVC-free textiles.
www.Dtex.com

Knoll
Textiles, seating and
products.www.knoll.com

FLOORING

Abaca
Banana fiber flooring.
www.laminart.com

Earth Weave
Sustainable flooring.
www.EarthWeave.com

Expanko Cork
Cork and rubber flooring.
www.expanko.com

Forbo
Sustainable flooring.
www.forbo-flooring.com

Fritz Tile
Post-consumer, recycled glass.
www.fritztile.com

Marmoleum
Natural linoleum.
www.themarmoleumstore.com

Natural Cork
Cork and bamboo flooring.
www.naturalcork.com

Plyboo
Bamboo flooring and cabinets.
www.plyboo.com

Warmboard
Radiant-heat subfloor.
www.warmboard.com

FURNITURE

Furnature
Furniture with organic cotton
upholstery.
www.furnature.com

Harmony in Design
Sustainable, handwoven
natural-fiber furniture.
www.harmonyindesign.com

HEAT, AIR CONDITIONING, VENTILATION AND WATER HEATERS

Grundfos
Instant hot-water service.
www.hotwaterrecirc.com

Rinnai America Corporation
Tankless water heaters.
www.rinnai.us

Takagi
Tankless water heaters.
www.takagi.com

INSULATION

Gaco Green
Reducing carbon footprint
with nontoxic insulation.
www.gaco.com/greensolutions.html

Icynene
Formaldehyde-free foam insulation.
www.icynene.com

Johns Manville
Formaldehyde-free fiberglass.
www.jmhomeinsulation.com

UltraTouch
Insulation made with
recycled denim and cotton fibers.
www.bondedlogic.com

LIGHTING

Gaiam LED and CFL lights
www.gaiam.com/retail/3/bulbs

SUSTAINABLE WOOD

EcoTimber
Eco-friendly flooring and decking.
www.ecotimber.com

Forest Stewardship Council
Sustainably harvested wood.
www.fscus.org

WALL COVERINGS AND PAINTS

AFM Safecoat
Zero- and low-VOC finishes.
www.AFMSafecoat.com

American Clay
Earth plaster.
www.americanclay.com

American Pride Paint
Eco-friendly paints.
www.americanpridepaint.com

Auro
Natural paints and plasters.
www.auroUSA.com

Best Paint:
Zero-VOC, low-odor paints.
www.bestpaintco.com

BioShield Paint
Clay paints and plasters, milk paints
and color washes.
www.bioshieldpaintco.com

Olivetti Mineral Finishes, LLC
Mineral-based paint.
www.olivettimineralfinishes.com

Yolo Colorhouse
Eco-friendly paint.
www.yolocolorhouse.com

WINDOWS, DOORS AND SKYLIGHTS

Andersen Windows
Low-E glass.
www.andersenwindows.com

Loewen Window & Door
Low-E windows.
www.loewen.com

Solatube
Energy Star skylights.
www.solatube.com

Velux Skylights
Energy Star skylights.
www.veluxUSA.com

WINDOW TREATMENTS

Designtex
PVC-free shades and screens.
www.Dtex.com

EarthShade
Green window fashions.
www.earthshade.com

MechoShade Systems
Solar window shades.
www.mechoshade.com

Books

Ray C. Anderson, *Mid-course Correction: Toward a Sustainable Enterprise: The Interface Model* (Atlanta: Peregrinzilla Press, 1999).

Annie Berthold-Bond, *Clean and Green: The Complete Guide to Non-Toxic and Environmentally Safe Housekeeping* (Woodstock, NY: Ceres Press 1994).

Debra Lynn Dadd, *Nontoxic & Natural: How to Avoid Dangerous Everyday Products and Buy or Make Safe Ones* (Los Angeles: Jeremy P. Teacher, Inc., 1984).

Burials

Web Sites and Organizations

Eternal Reefs
Patented mold systems developed to create reefs out of environmentally friendly concrete and cremation remains that closely mimic natural reef formations that are added to existing and/or deteriorating reefs to help improve the sea-life habitat.
www.eternalreefs.com.

Other Companies and Green Cemeteries

www.foreverfernwood.com/flash/index.html

www.greenburials.org

www.memorialecosystems.com

Business

Web Sites and Organizations

Bainbridge Graduate Institute
MBA and certificate programs in sustainable business.
www.bgiedu.org

Climate Counts
Green business rating system.
www.climatecounts.org

Climate Neutral Network
Improving the climate of doing business.
www.climateneutralnetwork.org

Co-Op America
Economic action for a just planet.
www.coopamerica.org

Cradle to Cradle Certification (C_2C)
High standard for environmentally intelligent design.
www.C_2Ccertified.com

Environmentally Responsible Mutual Funds
www.greencentury.com/greeninvesting

Green Dimes
Stop junk mail now, plant trees, save the planet.
www.greendimes.com

Green Investing
Guide to Responsible Investing.
www.care2.com/financial

GreenMoney Journal
Encourages and promotes the awareness of socially and environmentally
responsible business, investing and
consumer resources.
www.greenmoneyjournal.com

LEED (Leadership in Energy and
Environmental Design)
Certification and guidelines for
homes, businesses, buildings
and renovations.
www.usgbc.org

Indigo Financial Group
Specializes in energy-efficient
mortgages.
www.energyefficientmortgages.com

Greenlight Financial Services
www.greenlightloans.com

Energy Star Loans
www.energystarloans.com

Natural Step
Guide for companies, communities and governments onto an
ecologically, socially and
economically sustainable path.
www.naturalstep.org

Sustainable Business
www.sustainablebusiness.com/
progressiveinvestor

Sustainable Industries
Business news for organic food,
recycling, green building and
clean-energy industries.
www.sijournal.com

Books

Jill Bamburg. *Getting to Scale: Growing
Your Business Without Selling Out.*
(San Francisco: Berrett-Koehler
Publishing, 2006).

Clothing

Web Sites and Organizations

Blue Canoe
Organic cotton lifestyle clothing.
www.bluecanoe.com

Eco Baby
www.ecobaby.com

Gaiam
Organic cotton products from a
company dedicated to responsibility,
wellness and personal development.
www.gaiam.com

Green for Baby
www.greenforbaby.com

Green Loop
Eco fashion for men and women.
www.thegreenloop.com

Our Green House
www.ourgreenhouse.com

Patagonia
Clothing made from organic
cotton and recycled materials. Yvon
Chouinard's brainchild, the company
is dedicated to inspire and implement
solutions to the environmental crisis.
www.patagonia.com

Prana
Outdoor and yoga clothing made
from organic materials.
www.prana.com

Community

Web sites and Organizations

Curitiba, Brazil
A community with exceptional transportation, social inclusion, education and other environmental and social programs.
www.cdsea.org/db/knowledge.asp?ID=143
www.dismantle.org/curitiba.htm

The Earth Charter Initiative
A declaration of fundamental principles developed by the World Commission on Environment and Development for building a just, sustainable and peaceful global society for the twenty-first century.
www.earthcharter.org

Eco City Builders
Nonprofit dedicated to reshaping cities and communities.
www.ecocitybuilders.org

Ecocycle
Working to build zero-waste communities.
www.ecocycle.org

Energy-efficient and zero-energy affordable housing:
www.eere.energy.gov/buildings/building_america/affordable_housing.html

Enterprise Community Partners
Building energy-efficient homes for low-income families.
www.enterprisecommunity.org
www.greencommunitiesonline.org

Green Communities Program
A five-step planning process through which communities can become more sustainable.
www.epa.gov/greenkit/index.htm

Habitat for Humanity
Building affordable housing.
www.habitat.org

Murie Center
Bringing people together to develop and implement innovative strategies for conserving wild places and wildlife.
www.muriecenter.org

Natural Resources Defense Council
Dedicated to protecting health and the environment.
www.nrdc.org

Smart Growth
www.epa.gov/smartgrowth
www.smartgrowth.org

Syracuse Cultural Workers
Celebrating community and helping to change humans' interaction with the earth.
www.syrculturalworkers.com/about.html

Teton Science Schools
Educating, training and inspiring students of all ages about the natural world.
www.tetonscience.org

Books

David C. Korten, *The Great Turning: From Empire to Earth Community* (San Francisco: Barrett-Koehler Publishers, Inc., Bloomfield, CT: Kumarian Press, 2006).

David Suzuki, *The Sacred Balance: Rediscovering our Place in Nature* (Vancouver, BC, Canada: Greystone Books, 1997).

Mark Roseland, *Toward Sustainable Communities: Resources for Citizens and Their Governments* (Gabriola Island, BC, Canada: New Society Publishers, 2005).

Paul Hawken, *Blessed Unrest: How the Largest Movement in the World Came into Being and Why No One Saw it Coming* (New York: Viking, 2007).

Stephanie Kaza, ed., *Hooked! Buddhist Writings on Greed, Desire, and the Urge to Consume* (Boston: Shambhala Publications, 2005).

Warren Karlenzig, *How Green is Your City? The SustainLane U.S. City Rankings* (Gabriola Island, BC, Canada: New Society Publishers, 2007). Visit www.howgreenisyourcity.com for more information.

Energy

Web Sites and Organizations

Alliance to Save Energy
www.ase.org

Alliant Energy Kids
powerhousekids.com

American Council for an Energy Efficient Economy
www.aceee.org

Children and Energy
A teaching guide.
www.energyhog.org/childrens

Clean and GreenSupporting development of renewable energies in American communities.
www.cleanandgreen.us

Consumer Federation of America
www.buyenergyefficient.org

Energy Star Program
www.energystar.gov

Green Power Magazine
Magazine of renewable-energy products and technology.
www.greenpowermagazine.com

Green Power Network
www.eere.energy.gov/greenpower/markets

GEOTHERMAL

Home Power Magazine
Solar, wind and hydro design and building.
www.homepower.com

National Renewable Energy Laboratory
www.nrel.gov

Northern California Solar Energy Association
www.norcalsolar.org

Northeast Sustainable Energy Association
www.nesea.org

Oregon Institute of Technology's Geo Heat Center
http://geoheat.oit.edu/

Resources by state:
http://geoheat.oit.edu/colres.htm

Rocky Mountain Institute
www.rmi.org

SOLAR

"Heat Your Water with the Sun"
a booklet by the U.S. Department of Energy:
www.nrel.gov/docs/fy04osti/34279.pdf

Nanosolar
Thin-film solar.
www.nanosolar.com

"Solar Hot water, Heating and Cooling Systems"
www.greenbuilder.com/sourcebook

Solar Living Institute
Green-building workshops.
www.solarliving.org

Suntech
Solar power company specializing
in high-performance poly and mono
crystalline modules.
www.suntech-power.com

www.aceee.org/consumerguide/
topwater.htm

www.toolbase.org/pdf/fieldevaluations/
SheaFinalReportOctober2003.pdf

WIND

American Wind Energy Association
www.awea.org/policy

University of North Dakota Energy
and Environmental Research Center
www.undeerc.org/wind

Wind Power Tutorial
www.geology.wisc.edu/geo411/
hasselman.html

U.S. Department of Energy
www.eere.energy.gov

Books

Michael Brower and Warren Leon,
*The Consumer's Guide to Effective
Environmental Choices: Practical
Advice from the Union of Concerned
Scientists* (New York: Three Rivers
Press, 1999).

Paul Scheckel, *The Home Energy Diet*
(Gabriola Island, BC, Canada: New
Society Publishers, 2005).

Alex Wilson and others, *Consumer
Guide to Home Energy Savings, 8th
Edition* (Washington D.C.: American
Council for an Energy-Efficient
Economy, 2003).

Food

Web Sites and Organizations

American Community
Gardening Association
Growing community through
gardening and greening.
www.communitygarden.org

Community Supported Agriculture
(CSA) www.localharvest.org/csa/
www.greenpeople.org/csa.htm

Composting
www.epa.gov/compost
www.vegweb.com/composting

Farmers markets across the country:
www.ams.usda.gov/farmersmarkets/
map.htm www.farmersmarket.com

Farm to School
Connecting schools with local farms
to serve healthy meals in school
cafeterias.
www.farmtoschool.org

Food First
Institute for food development
and policy.
www.foodfirst.org

Green Guerillas for Urban Food
Helping New York City create and
sustain community gardens.
www.greenguerillas.org

Land Institute
Developing ecologically
sustainable agriculture.
www.landinstitute.org

Marin Organic
An association of organic producers
in Marin County, California.
www.marinorganic.org

Organic Consumers
www.organicconsumers.org

Slow Food USA
A nonprofit dedicated to supporting locally grown food and combating fast food and "fast life."
www.slowfoodusa.org

Sustainable Research, Agriculture and Education
Providing grants to improve profitability, stewardship and quality of life.
www.sare.org/index.htm

Sustainable Table
An educational resource on healthy food choices.
www.sustainabletable.org

Water, drinking and bottled:
www.EPA.gov/safewater
www.allaboutwater.org/environment.html

Books and Magazines

Barbara Kingsolver, *Animal, Vegetable Miracle: A Year of Food Life* (New York: Harper Collins, 2007).

Daniel Imhoff, *Paper or Plastic: Searching for Solutions to an Overpackaged World* (San Francisco: Sierra Club Books, 2005).

Elizabeth Henderson, *Sharing the Harvest* (White River Junction, VT: Chelsea Green Publishing, 1999).

Farmer John Peterson and others, *Farmer John's Cookbook: The Real Dirt on Vegetables* (Layton, UT: Gibbs Smith, Publisher, 2006).

Steve Petusevsky and others, *The Whole Foods Market Cookbook: A Guide to Natural Foods with 350 Recipes* (New York: Clarkson Potter Publishers, 2002).

Touch the Soil
Saving civilization's roots.
www.touchthesoil.com

Fish and Seafood

Sea Choice
Canada's sustainable seafood.
www.seachoice.org

Seafood Watch
Make choices for healthy seafood consumption with a downloadable seafood guide by region.
www.mbayaq.org/cr/cr_seafood-watch/download.asp

Gardening and Lawn Care

Web sites and Organizations

Beyond Pesticides
National coalition about the misuse of pesticides.
www.beyondpesticides.org

Colorado State University's extension program
Xeriscaping, landscape design and organic gardening.
www.ext.colostate.edu/index

Colorado Water Wise Community
www.xeriscape.org

"Grasscycling" to reduce waste from lawns:
www.fcgov.com/recycling/basics.php

High Country Gardens
Xeriscaping plants.
www.highcountrygardens.com

Lawns and lawn-care tips:
www.american-lawns.com

Natural Lawn Care
www.eartheasy.com/grow_lawn_care.htm

Organic gardening resource:
www.organicgardening.com

Rainwater Harvesting Systems
www.conservationtechnology.com

Seeds of Change
Organic seeds and food.
www.seedsofchange.com

Sustainable Gardening

www.recycleworks.org/compost/
sustainable_gardening.html

Sustainable growth:
www.sustainablegrowth.com

Sustainable lawn care:
www.sustland.umn.edu/maint/
maint.htm

Global Warming

Web Sites and Organizations

California Climate Change Portal
News releases and information on
climate change and greenhouse gas
emissions.
www.climatechange.ca.gov

Cities for Climate Protection
www.iclei.org/co2

Conservation International
International nonprofit conserving
biodiversity.
www.conservation.org

European Environmental Bureau
A federation of over 140 European
Union environmental groups.
www.eeb.org

Greenpeace
www.greenpeace.org/usa

International Council for
Local Environmental Initiatives
www.iclei.org

Pew Center on Global Climate Change
www.pewclimate.org

Sir Nicholas Stern Review of
the Economics of Climate Change
www.hm-treasury.gov.uk/

independent_reviews/stern_review_
economics_climate_change/stern
review_index.cfm

Step It Up
Writer and activist Bill McKibben's
charge to organize actions for
global-warming awareness.
www.stepitup2007.org

Union of Concerned Scientists
Climate change, clean fuel, GMOs
and other issues.
www.UCSUSA.org

U.S. Mayors Climate Protection
Agreement
U.S. communities taking action
to reduce global warming.
www.seattle.gov/mayor/climate

World Conservation Union
Also known as the International
Union for the Conservation of Nature
and Natural Resources, the world's
largest conservation network.
www.iucn.org

World Wildlife Federation
Building awareness about global
warming, endangered species, wildlife
conservation and animal habitats.
www.worldwildlife.org

Books

Al Gore, *An Inconvenient Truth* (New
York: Rodale, Inc., and Viking, 2006).

Chris Goodall, *How to Live a Low-
Carbon Life: The Individual's Guide to
Stopping Climate Change* (Sterling,
VA: Earthscan, 2007).

David Gershon, *Low Carbon Diet: A 30-Day Program to Lose 5,000 Pounds* (Woodstock, NY: Empowerment Institute, 2006).

David Suzuki and Holly Dressel, *Good News For a Change: How Everyday People Are Helping the Planet* (Vancouver, BC, Canada: Greystone Books, 2002).

James Howard Kunstler, *The Long Emergency: Surviving the End of Oil, Climate Change, and Other Converging Catastrophes of the Twenty-First Century* (New York: Grove Press, 2005).

Lester R. Brown, *Plan B: Rescuing a Planet Under Stress and a Civilization in Trouble* (New York: W. W. Norton & Company, 2003).

Ross Gelpspan, *The Heat Is On: The Climate Crisis, the Cover-up, the Prescription* (Jackson, TN: Perseus Books Group, 1997).

Hospitals and Schools

Web Sites and Organizations

The Green Schools Initiative
www.greenschools.net/index.html

Hospitals for a Healthy Environment (H2E)
Creating a national movement for environmental sustainability in health care.
www.h2e-online.org/

Sierra Environmental
Nontoxic commercial cleaners.
www.calsave.org/companies/sierraenv/

The Sustainable Schools Project
A model for schools that want to use sustainability to improve curriculum

and civic engagement.
www.sustainableschoolsproject.org

Top Ten Green Hospitals in the United States, 2006:
www.thegreenguide.com/doc/113/top 10hospitals

Films

The 11th Hour (2007)
Interviews with over fifty leading scientists, thinkers and leaders who discuss the state of the world and the state of humanity.
http://11thhourfilm.com/

An Inconvenient Truth (2006)
Former Vice President Al Gore's view of the future of our planet.
www.climatecrisis.net

Crude Impact (2006)
Explores the interconnection between human domination of the planet and the discovery and use of oil.
www.crudeimpact.com

Everything's Cool (2007)
A handful of global-warming "messengers" speak out in a "toxic comedy" about global-warming coming to America.
www.everythingscool.org

Fast Food Nation (2006)
An ensemble piece examining the health risks involved in the fast-food industry and its environmental and social consequences.
www.fastfoodnation-movie.com/trailer.php

The Future of Food (2004)
Overview of the key questions raised by consumers as they become aware of genetically modified foods.
www.thefutureoffood.com/

The Power of Community (2006)
How Cuba survived peak oil. Cuba provides a valuable example of how to successfully address the challenge of reducing our energy use.
www.powerofcommunity.org/cm/index.php

The Real Dirt on Farmer John (2006)
A whimsical profile of the organic farmer John.
www.farmerjohnmovie.com/Home.html

Who Killed the Electric Car? (2006)
Documentary film that explores the birth, limited commercialization and subsequent death of the battery electric vehicle in the United States, specifically the General Motors EV1 of the 1990s.
www.whokilledtheelectriccar.com

Magazines and Webzines

Audubon Magazine
www.audubonmagazine.org

David Suzuki Foundation and Science Matters column:
www.davidsuzuki.org

Delicious Living Magazine
www.deliciouslivingmag.com

E, the Environmental Magazine
www.emagazine.com

Global Green and Green Cross International
USA and global organizations dedicated to researching, educating and funding in hopes of creating a "sustainable and secure future."
www.globalgreen.org/index.html
www.gci.ch/en/about/mission.htm

Good Magazine
Magazine for people who "give a damn."
www.goodmagazine.com

The Green Guide
www.thegreenguide.com/issue.mhtml?i=113

Greenlight Magazine
Guide to earth-friendly living.
www.greenlightmag.com/magazine.php

Greentips by Union of Concerned Scientists
Group working for a healthy environment and a safer world.
www.ucsusa.org/publications/greentips

Green Home Living Magazine
www.greenhome.com/info/magazine

Grist Magazine
Environmental news and commentary.
www.grist.org

Headwaters News
Commentary and reporting on issues of the Rocky Mountain West.
www.headwatersnews.org

High Country News
News magazine that reports on the West's natural resources, public lands and changing communities.
www.hcn.org

Mother Jones Magazine
Social and environmental justice.
www.motherjones.com

Natural Home Magazine
Earth-inspired living in print and on the Web.
www.naturalhomemagazine.com

Nau
Sustainable clothing company dedicated to social and environmental change with a daily updated blog and reader-generated video, photography and editorial content.
www.nau.com

Orion Magazine and Orion Society
www.orionmagazine.org

Terra Pass Newsletter
Organization preventing global warming, reducing carbon dioxide pollution and promoting renewable energy.
www.terrapass.com

TreeHugger
Green news from the United Kingdom.
www.treehugger.com

Yes! Magazine
www.yesmagazine.org

Office/Home Office

Computer Take-Back Campaign
Recycling your computer.
www.computertakeback.org

Dolphin Blue
Environmentally friendly office supplies.
www.dolphinblue.com

Energy-efficient lighting for offices:
www.wbdg.org/design/efficient
lighting.php

The Green Office
Online retailer of recycled, environmentally friendly and sustainable business products, school supplies and paper.
www.thegreenoffice.com

Greenline Paper Company
Recycled paper for home and office.
www.greenlinepaper.com

Herman Miller
Nontoxic, ergonomically designed office furniture.
www.hermanmiller.com

How to Green Your Office
A United Kingdom site with ideas, products and cleaning material.

www.greenyouroffice.co.uk

The Real Earth Company
Office supply store.
www.therealearth.com

Sustainable Group
Binders, paper and other supplies.
www.sustainablegroup.net

Treecycle
Recycled paper products.
www.treecycle.com/catintro.html

Twisted Limb Paper
www.twistedlimbpaper.com

Pet Care

Green Dog Pet Supply
Environmentally friendly pet supplies and gifts for dogs, cats and their people.
www.greendogpetsupply.com.

Holistic Food For Pets
Premium food, treats and supplements for dogs, cats and horses.
www.holisticfood4pets.biz

Only Natural Pet Store
Natural products, holistic remedies, organic food and more for dogs and cats.
www.onlynaturalpet.com

Purrfect Play
Pet toys crafted exclusively from organic, dye-free and chemical-free natural fibers.
www.purrfectplay.com

Recycling

Web Sites and Organizations

Earth911
City-by-city information on recycling

Freecycle
A forum for exchanging items for reuse.
www.freecycle.org

National Recycling Coalition
Promoting investment in residential
recycling programs.
www.nrc-recycle.org

U.S. Environmental Protection
Agency's recycling Web site:
www.epa.gov/msw/recycle.htm

Books

Fran Berman, *Trash to Cash: How
Businesses Can Save Money and
Increase Profits* (Boca Raton, FL:
CRC, 1996).

Rhonda Lucas Donald, *Recycling* (New
York: Barnes & Noble, Children's
Press CT, 2002).

Transportation

Web Sites and Organizations

Anti-Idling in Canada
www.oee.nrcan.gc.ca/communities-
government/idling.cfm?attr=8
www.mississauga.ca/portal/residents/
idlefree

Anti-Idling Primer
www.thehcf.org/antiidlingprimer.html

Carbon offset programs from around
the world:
www.cdmgoldstandard.org

Carbon offset programs in Canada:
www.pollutionprobe.com
www.cooldrivepass.com

Carbon offset programs in Europe:
www.carbonneutral.com

Carbon offset programs
in the United States:
www.eere.energy.gov/greenpower/
markets/certificates.shtml?page=1
www.green-e.org

Clean Car Campaign
www.cleancarcampaign.org

Cleaning up city fleets:
www.eere.energy/gov/fleetguide

Electric Bike
Electric power and pedaling.
www.ecozen.com/bike1.htm

European Federation for Transport
and the Environment
www.transportenvironment.org

Green Car Congress
Energy, technologies, issues and
policies for sustainable mobility
www.greencarcongress.com

Green transportation links:
www.rainforestweb.org/What_You_
Can_Do/Green_Transportation

How to make your own biodiesel:
www.journeytoforever.org/biodiesel_
make.html
www.biodieselcommunity.org

Hydrogen-compressed natural gas
busses:
www.greencarcongress.com/2007/06/
translink-puts-.html

National Biodiesel Board
www.biodiesel.org

Offset your carbon footprint:
www.b-e-f.org, www.myfootprint.com
www.nativeenergy.com
www.terraPass.com

Plug-in cars:
www.Calcars.org
www.pluginamerica.com
www.pluginbayarea.org

Plug-ins at truck stops:
www.eere.energy.gov/vehiclesandfuels
www.shurepower.com
www.idleaire.com

Rainforest Action's Campaign
for Cleaner Cars
www.RAN.org/what-we-do/freedom-
from-oil/

Rate the fuel economy of your vehicle:
www.fueleconomy.gov

Salt Lake City Light Rail Study
Integration testing of starting up a
light rail system.
www.arema.org/eseries/scriptcontent
/custom/e_arema/library/2000_
Conference_Proceedings/00054.pdf

Solar Electrical Vehicles
www.solarelectricalvehicles.com

Solar Trike
Three-wheeled creative alternative
to a vehicle.
www.solartrike.com

Transportation Alternatives
Cycling, walking and environmentally
sensible transportation.
www.transalt.org/index.html

Zip Cars
Car sharing in various cities.
www.zipcar.com

Books

Amory B. Lovins, *Winning the Oil
Endgame* (Rocky Mountain
Institute, 2007). For more
information, visit
www.oilendgame.com.

David Freeman, *Winning Our Energy
Independence: An Energy Insider
Shows How* (Layton, Utah: Gibbs
Smith, Publisher, 2007).

Geoffrey B. Holland, *The Hydrogen
Age: Empowering A Clean-Energy
Future* (Layton, Utah, Gibbs Smith,
Publisher, 2007).

Jeremy Rifkin, *The Hydrogen Economy*
(New York: Jeremy P. Tarcher/
Putnam, 2002).

Katie Alvord, *Divorce Your Car:
Ending the Love Affair with the
Automobile* (Gabriola Island, BC,
Canada: New Society Publishers,
2000).

Sherry Boschert, *Plug-in Hybrids*
(Gabriola Island, BC, Canada: New
Society Publishers, 2006).

Water

Web Sites and Organizations

USGS Water Basics for Schools
http://ga.water.usgs.gov/edu/mwater.
html

Water Conservation Portal
& Search Engine
www.waterconserve.info

WaterPartners International
Working to get safe drinking water to
people worldwide.
www.water.org

World Water Council
www.worldwatercouncil.org

Women's Health and Personal Care

Web Sites and Organizations

Campaign for Safe Cosmetics
www.safecosmetics.org

Earth Mama Angel Baby
One hundred percent natural skin- and body-care products and gifts that support the entire process from childbirth to natural baby care.
www.earthmamaangelbaby.com

Environmental Working Group
Investigating threats to health.
www.ewg.org

Health Care without Harm
www.noharm.org

Impact Analysis
Environmental health Web log.
http://impact_analysis.blogspot.com/

June Russell's Health Facts
information on health from antioxidants to pesticides.
www.jrussellshealth.org

Physicians for Social Responsibility
www.psr.org

Precautionary Principle
The Science and Environmental Health Network is working to implement this principle, which states that if an action or policy might cause severe or irreversible harm to the public, it should be avoided.
www.sehn.org/precaution.html

PVC, The Poison Plastic
www.pvcfree.org

Savvy Patients
Information on treatments, facilities and medicine.
www.savvypatients.com

Tiny Footprints
Tips for raising healthy children in a healthy environment.
www.tinyfootprints.org

University of Pittsburgh Center for Environmental Oncology
www.environmentaloncology.org

Women's Health
www.womenshealthandthe environment.org

Women's Voices for the Earth
www.womenandenvironment.org

Books

Devra Davis, *The Secret History of the War on Cancer* (New York: Basic Books, 2007)

Tampons and Tampon Alternatives

Diva Cup:
www.divacup.com

Natracare:
www.natracare.com

Sea sponge tampons:
www.seapearls.co.uk

Diapers

gDiapers
Flushable diapers with no elemental chlorine, perfumes, smell or garbage.
www.gdiapers.com

Nature Boy and Girl's Healthy Baby Diaper, LLC
Disposable diaper brand.
www.natureboyandgirl.net.

Seventh Generation
Chlorine-free diapers.
www.seventhgeneration.com

Index